Just Say "Good Dog"

—— Teaching the Family Dog ——

TS-204

Distributed in the UNITED STATES to the Pet Trade by T.F.H. Publications, Inc., One T.F.H. Plaza, Neptune City, NJ 07753; distributed in the UNITED STATES to the Bookstore and Library Trade by National Book Network, Inc. 4720 Boston Way, Lanham MD 20706; in CANADA to the Pet Trade by H & L Pet Supplies Inc., 27 Kingston Crescent, Kitchener, Ontario N2B 2T6; Rolf C. Hagen Ltd., 3225 Sartelon Street, Montreal 382 Quebec; in CANADA to the Book Trade by Macmillan of Canada (A Division of Canada Publishing Corporation), 164 Commander Boulevard, Agincourt, Ontario M1S 3C7; in the United Kingdom by T.F.H. Publications, PO Box 15, Waterlooville PO7 6BQ; in AUSTRALIA AND THE SOUTH PACIFIC by T.F.H. (Australia), Pty. Ltd., Box 149, Brookvale 2100 N.S.W., Australia; in NEW ZEALAND by Brooklands Aquarium Ltd. 5 McGiven Drive, New Plymouth, RD1 New Zealand; in Japan by T.F.H. Publications, Japan—Jiro Tsuda, 10-12-3 Ohjidai, Sakura, Chiba 285, Japan; in SOUTH AFRICA by Multipet Pty. Ltd., P.O. Box 35347, Northway, 4065, South Africa. Published by T.F.H. Publications, Inc.
Manufactured in the United States of America
by T.F.H. Publications, Inc.

Just Say "Good Dog"

—— *Teaching the Family Dog* ——

Linda Goodman

with
Marlene Trunnell

Illustrations by AnnMarie Freda

Contents

About the Author

Linda Goodman was born in Stratford, Connecticut. Her first dog was a little black cross breed whom she named Midnite.

After graduating from the University of Connecticut, she moved to Schenectady, New York to work for General Electric. There she acquired another black cross breed—Porgy. In 1969, Linda moved to California to work for TRW and Porgy came with her.

Porgy died in 1983. To ease the pain, she became a member of the board of directors for the West End Shelter for Animals in Ontario, CA—a great way to learn about animal care, behavior and people.

During her two years on the board, Linda coordinated a volunteer program, pet adoption counseling, pet bereavement counseling and pet visits to hospitals and nursing homes.

She completed and taught pet bereavement counseling classes and was general manager of a boarding kennel in Garden Grove.

Linda has owned and taught dogs for most of her life and traveled from San Diego to San Francisco to consult with and learn from veterinarians, animal behaviorists and humane groups.

In 1986 she struck out on her own to start **P.O.R.G.I.E.** (**P**et **O**wnership **R**equires **G**etting **I**nformed and **E**ducated) and now has her own teaching center in Riverside, CA.

Linda's humane and enjoyable methods of teaching puppy/dogs and their people have earned the respect of professionals and pet lovers alike.

Dedication

To two very special dogs. Porgy, without your death I would never have travelled this path. In life you were my savior and in death you still guide me. Paige, you are my teacher and my healer. Your life helps me to continue on the path of learning, teaching and healing.

Acknowledgments

I don't believe any book can be written entirely by one person. We are all a composite of our experiences. Everyone we meet in the journey we call life affects us in some way. I cannot thank everyone I have ever met by name; I do not remember the names of everyone I have ever met. However, some names do come to mind: Freda Katzoff, who has been a friend, a teacher and an inspiration to always be the best person I can be. Donna O'Shaughnessy, who has taught me what friendship and loyalty mean. Ian Dunbar, who gave me my first exposure to the concepts of puppy teaching with his workshops. Jeannie Collins, who inspires me to smile and introduced me to William Campbell, a man I had admired from afar. Sue Myles, who made a constant effort to bring like minds together. Betty Fryman, who opened up new worlds and possibilities for me when I really needed it. The students, both two-legged and four-legged, who attend my classes and encourage me to write and teach.

I must also thank my dear friend Marlene Trunnell without whom this book would never have been written. She gave me the courage and the support to do all of this. The hours of dedication, reading and re-reading every word until we had it right, are a memory I treasure. We laughed, we argued, we joked, we learned from each other, we shared and we loved every minute of it.

I also want to thank my husband Joseph Findeis for his love and his patience during the time it took to write this. My life was incomplete until I met him and learned the power of love. Of course I must also thank my pets Porgy, Toby, Paige, Tribune, Bacchus, Katzie, Sibur, Hunka and Shenanigan, who have taught me more about life, love and the universe than I could ever teach them.

"Let's Stop Choking Dogs": An Introduction

This is a book about *teaching* dogs. Teaching them words without using choke chains, collars, leashes or punishments so that they can live in the house with the family. A book different from any other on the subject. Books by individuals involved in the sport of showing dogs always demand too much of pet people—too much time, too much perfection, too much discipline and too much precision. Most other books either tell owners how to train with a choke chain or how to punish instead of reward; give only part of the training techniques but without enough detail; or are aimed at obedience trial training.

Pet people are not usually interested in obedience trials. They don't care if a sit is straight or crooked. I remember the first time I attended an obedience class with my dog. I said **Sit** and my dog actually sat. I was so excited I was ready to do yippy-ya-ha dances in the street. I had actually communicated a message and been understood. The instructor was shouting, "Make that dog sit straight!" and I looked around to see who was being yelled at—imagine my surprise when it turned out to be me. The trainer took that successful moment and turned it into a failure just because it was not a perfect sit by obedience standards! He really took the fun out of training my dog!

My dog was not going to be a show dog or compete in obedience trials. I just wanted to enjoy him as a companion. It is very difficult to find classes or books for pet people. That is why I started to teach my classes as "pet people education" courses. I do not even use the word Heel in my classes!

Most books on dogs are written by obedience instructors for people interested in competing in obedience trials. I assure you this book is written by and for another pet person. It is about teaching a dog to be a family member. Pet people want a family dog to enjoy—the teaching should be fun, not tedious; the dog should be under control, not a robot; we must learn to understand and communicate, not just command.

Sometimes we humans forget that the teaching of words must be done in order to communicate. You don't have to teach your dog how to **Sit, Down, Come, Stay** or **Walk**—he already knows how to do all of these things. Your job is to teach him words that mean these behaviors so you can communicate with him. Teach him that your words have meaning and what it feels like to succeed, and you teach him how to learn.

Imagine yourself living in a foreign country where you don't speak the language and people are ordering you around and hitting you for not doing as they say. You would love to do what they're telling you but you just don't understand their words. Why are they hitting you instead of helping you to understand? That is how your dog probably feels when you tell him to **Sit**, then pull on a choke chain and push on his rump! That hurts and it's certainly no fun!

Would you want to put a choke chain around the neck of a tiger, then teach him to **Sit** by pulling up on the choke chain and pushing down on his rump? I think not! No one would want to train a tiger with this technique—you wouldn't have a leg to stand on!

The only reason we get away with this method on the dog is because the dog lets us do it—he is probably the most forgiving animal on the planet Earth!

Of course each dog is a separate and unique individual, so it is wise to be aware of the dog's personality. Some boisterous pups will need a really loud voice for an effective reprimand and a quiet pup may need only a scowling look and a little, quiet growl. If your puppy overreacts to loud noises, slowly build up his tolerance level. After all, life is full of loud noises—thunder, firecrackers, sirens, etc.—and he must learn not to be fearful. This book is aimed at the average puppy who will not become a wiggly, piddling little worm if you are overexuberant with your praise and instructive reprimands.

This book also will take a look at life from the dog's point of view. All dogs are urinating, defecating, biting, barking, chewing, digging, jumping machines. Usually these doggy behaviors are defined as problems from the human point of view; but, from the dog's point of view, they are natural—they are what define him as a dog and not an elephant!

To try to stop the dog from behaving like a dog is totally unfair. *Properly defining* the problem allows you to solve the problem and still let the dog do his doggy things. Very often the poor dog misinterprets the intended rule and appears to willfully misbehave. Being aware of the dog's point of view can really help when you're teaching your puppy or troubleshooting a problem.

For example, if your dog is jumping around at feeding time and you place his food bowl in front of him, you're rewarding him for all the jumping and teaching him to behave like a kangaroo for his meal. From the dog's point of view, if he is fed while jumping, it would probably appear as if you really enjoy the chaos surrounding feeding time—after all, you reward him with one of the greatest thrills of the day, his meal! If, instead, you teach him to **Sit** before he is rewarded with his food, a toy, a caress or anything he may want or need, he will respect you, learn to look to you for leadership and be calmer because he knows a better way to behave.

Another example is chewing. You don't have to stop him from chewing because chewing is not the real problem—the problem is what the dog "chewses" to chew. When the puppy chews your slippers it's no problem to him—actually it was quite enjoyable and helped pass the time. The problem is from your point of view. You see him as a destructive little monster who may not live to celebrate his next birthday! Therefore, it is up to you to teach him what he can and cannot chew in your home!

When you have a problem with your dog, try to remember the dog is doing the best he can under the given circumstances. If he continuously does something wrong and you insistently use the same approach, you never solve the problem. He has a point of view and can only respond based on how he interprets the information you give him.

If what you try to teach has not made a difference by the third or fourth time you have tried it, then it probably *won't* work. Humans insist on repeating the same technique over and over again even though it gets no results, convinced the dog will finally understand or that he is "too stupid to train."

Too many dogs live their lives in the backyard because the owner is focused on what the dog does wrong and ways to punish him. All too often the question asked is "How can I *break* my dog of his bad habits?" Instead, the question should be "What am *I* doing that causes the dog to misbehave in this manner?"

The problem is that you are not communicating

the message you intend and the dog is responding to the message he thinks you are sending. If you would reward the dog when he does something right, you would probably solve the problem much more easily and quickly. People would like their dogs better if they would recognize how much the dog does that is right. Instead of ignoring good behavior, "reward" it so it will be repeated.

The best time to start teaching any dog is as soon as possible! It is a shame that obedience trainers still insist that owners must wait until a dog is at least six months to teach him anything. That is the silliest bit of rubbish! The owner is wasting valuable time and missing out on the opportunity to create a socialized, confident, temperamentally sound family dog who would be safe indoors around other pets, young children, and visitors. At six months the animal has the body, strength and teeth of an adult dog and the mind of a "rebellious teenager"!

Actually, teaching begins the moment you bring

your new dog home. Everything you do with your pet is a learning experience for both of you. In computer lingo they always say "Garbage in/Garbage out!" This is especially true with the puppy. The puppy's brain is like a blank computer disk and all of your interactions help to fill up the disk with new information. To input the appropriate behavior for life amongst humans, the dog and you will benefit most by living together.

Dogs are sociable and belong in the home with the family. The only way to derive the many benefits of having a dog is by living with the dog.

Outdoor dogs live an unnatural life because they are social creatures deprived of social interactions. Being alone each and every day is like a sentence of solitary confinement for life—a most severe form of punishment. Imagine yourself kept in one room all the time, day after day. The only time you see another person is when someone comes in daily to leave you food and water and clean up your waste. You'd go batty! Your behavior might become very destructive and you would probably try to escape your dull and boring environment. That one brief moment when a person entered your room would be the highlight of your day. You'd want to joyously greet her, hug her, be hugged back and have some conversation, anything that would prolong the visit and end the eternal solitude.

Your exuberant delight might be offensive to your keeper but your joy at not being alone would be uncontrollable. The visits would probably become shorter and shorter because your behavior is so offensive to your keeper and you would become crazier and crazier. That is how a dog may feel if he has to live all alone in the yard!

This book is aimed at teaching very young puppies to live in the home as family members by using

positive techniques. However, I do use the same methods on puppies and dogs, and find them to be extremely effective and lots of fun, regardless of the dog's age. Anything that can be done with a puppy can be done with a dog and visa versa. Therefore, the terms puppy and dog are used interchangeably throughout this book.

I have created a fictitious dog named SEBASTIAN who will be used as the demonstration dog. Wherever you see his name, mentally replace it with the name of your dog.

Make A Commitment To Your Dog

Bringing any pet into the family is not a decision to make lightly. The family must be 100% committed to this new family member. Family pets need more than just food, water and shelter. Adopting a dog requires a commitment that must last for 10 to 15 years or more.

Commitments are much easier to keep when you have guidelines. This is especially true when you bring a dog into the family. The family and the dog must have guidelines if they are to live happily together. The following are some suggested guidelines for carrying through on your commitment to your dog:

1. The family pet should always be spayed or neutered. It's the kind and caring thing to do. We do *not* need more dogs born to die.

2. Obtaining a dog should be an unanimous family decision.

3. Adults in the family are ultimately responsible for the dog even if he was bought "for the children."

4. Everyone in the family must be consistent. Inconsistency leads to confusion and confusion leads to unacceptable behavior.

5. Be aware of the laws in your community that apply to pets and *obey* them.

6. The dog should always wear a properly fitting buckle collar with current identification information.

7. Never take your dog off your property without a leash. A dog off-leash is at more risk than a dog on-leash.

8. If you can no longer keep your pet you must find him a new home or take him to the animal shelter. It is inhumane to abandon or dump an animal. Even the worst shelter is far better than a horrible street death.

9. Never hit or in any way abuse your animal.

10. Start teaching your dog the moment you bring him home!

11. Use crates, barriers, etc., to set limits so the dog succeeds rather than fails. Too much freedom too soon is a frequent mistake.

12. Keep teaching sessions interesting, fun and short—five minutes at most, several times a day. Always end a session with the dog having succeeded. That way both of you can look forward to the next session.

13. Slower can be faster. When you try to progress too quickly during teaching you can actually slow the learning process.

14. When a "mistake" occurs, step back and try to determine what *you* are doing wrong. A new approach may be necessary to help the dog understand what you want!

15. Don't expect your dog to behave like a four-legged human being. All the dog is capable of being is a dog. He sees the world from a dog's point of view and that is usually different from a human's point of view!

16. Be aware of the dog's point of view and know exactly what you are teaching him to do. Every interaction is a teaching session for your puppy.

17. Praise your dog when he is well behaved. He repeats those behaviors that draw attention to him. Being yelled at is better than being ignored. Being praised when he is right is definitely better than being yelled at!

18. Make every interaction with your puppy a chance to teach him something. Anything your dog wants or needs can be used as a reward. Take advantage of this.

19. Teach your puppy the meaning of your words before you use them as commands. Instead of obedience training try *teaching* your dog as you would a child.

20. Take the time to teach your dog that your words have meaning. Use these words in your everyday life to teach him the rules of being a well-behaved family member.

21. Teach your dog the basic command words—**Off, Sit, Come, Walk, Down, Stay.** Commands can save your dog's life in an emergency.

22. Your dog's name is not a command and should

not be said in a negative tone. His name is an attention getting device and he should respond happily when he hears it.

23. Never call your dog to you for anything the dog may perceive as negative or punishing.

24. *No one* should ever play tug-of-war with a dog who has not been taught the rules of biting.

25. Never feed your dog from the table. Always place food in his bowl and let him eat at his usual location.

26. Fresh water must always be available for your dog.

27. Your dog should be fed a high quality food and fresh fruits and vegetables—not table scraps or generic dog food.

28. Puppies require a series of vaccinations until they are four months old. Then they receive their last puppy shot and a rabies shot.

29. Never delay veterinary attention for a sick animal. In some cases, time may mean the difference between life and death.

30. Keep your dog and his environment clean and free of internal and external parasites.

31. You must teach your dog the rules of the house so he can live in the home with the family. Dogs are social animals and need to be part of a group. (If you don't want your dog in your home, maybe you really don't want a dog!)

32. Love and respect your dog. One of the most common reasons for obtaining a dog is the *unconditional love* they give. Try to do the same for your dog. It's the least you can do for a friend!

33. A small child and a dog should never be left unattended—a responsible adult should *always* be present when they are together.

34. Never allow a small child and your dog to be on the floor together. The child should be in a chair if the dog is in the same room. If the child wants to play on

the floor it is preferable for her to play in her room.

35. When children and dogs are living together, the dog must be taught to tolerate rough handling and teasing without biting and the children must be taught never to tease or be abusive with the dog.

36. Puppies, like children, need undisturbed rest periods during the day.

37. Never leave your dog in a parked car—regardless of the weather. The inside of a car can heat up very quickly and endanger the well-being of the dog.

38. When travelling with your dog, never allow him to ride with his head out the window or to rattle around in the bed of a pickup truck. Be sure he is seated inside or safely secured at all times.

39. If you have a problem with your dog, do not ignore it. Problems do not go away, they must be solved.

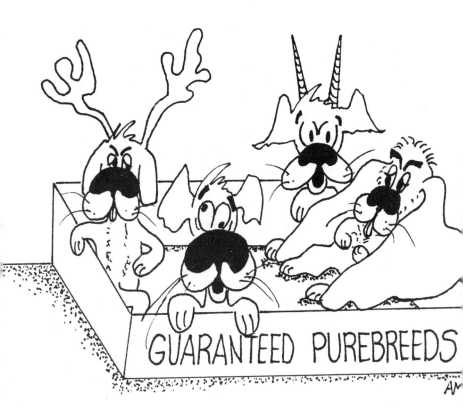

To Breed Or Not To Breed?

Before I proceed with teaching techniques and problem solving, there is a subject of utmost importance that must be addressed—the spaying and neutering of pets. Many people close their minds to the facts about this issue but in order to make good, informed decisions you must know the facts.

Millions of animals die every year in America because there are not enough good homes for them. Breeding is out of control and it's the animals who suffer. Why is this happening? One reason is the puppy mills. These are breeding factories where puppies are born, weaned as soon as possible, packaged and shipped all over the country. These puppies are usually of inferior health and quality, sometimes not even true purebreds. Their temperaments are usually very "bitey." They're unsocialized and very often "gotten rid of" because owners find it impossible to live with them.

The mills are only a small part of the problem. The more serious factor that must be addressed is backyard breeders. They know nothing about responsible breeding. These people buy dogs from unscrupulous dealers or backyard breeders, pay an outrageous price, then want to "make money" by producing more puppies. But dogs are not mutual funds. They are living, breathing, feeling creatures and should not be exploited for monetary gains.

Most backyard breeders quickly learn that finding homes for their puppies is a very difficult task. If you have ever seen people giving away puppies in front of the supermarket, it is probably because they believed their friends when they said they would love to have a pup. They soon learned that once the puppies were a reality their friends had a multitude of excuses as to why this was not a good time for them to have a dog.

American shelters are full of purebred, AKC-registered dogs no one wants. A backyard breeder is anyone who breeds a dog, intentionally or unintentionally, to give puppies to friends, for the kids to experience the miracle of birth or to attempt to make money, with no regard for good breeding practices.

There is only one acceptable reason to breed dogs—to make a better dog, not just more dogs. There is only one reason not to spay or neuter and that is to *responsibly* breed. Ethical breeders don't breed to make money. They want to improve the breed's health, characteristics, temperament and abilities. They spend at least two years studying the breed, learning about genetics, attending breed club meetings, going to dog shows, meeting other responsible breeders and learning all they can about the breed *before* purchasing a dog to start a breeding program. It's very difficult to find responsible breeders willing to part with breeding stock to help someone start a breeding program. Before selling a puppy, they must be convinced of a sincere effort on the buyer's part to learn and study before undertaking this project.

A responsible breeder never breeds dogs under two years of age. It takes two years of development before the dog can be certified free of genetic disorders known to the breed. Ethical breeding would never be done without certifying the animals free of these problems.

A responsible breeder takes time off from work to be there when the female gives birth to the litter. This may sound silly, but all sorts of complications can occur when she's left alone. Very often the dog doesn't know what to do and puppies can be lost through her inexperience, and there is always the possibility of complications requiring veterinary attention.

The first three weeks of a puppy's life are pretty much in the care of the mother dog. During that time, and definitely after, the puppies should be handled by humans to get them accustomed to human touch, smell, sounds, etc. Each pup should be taken separately from the litter and temperament tested.

Records should be kept on each pup's reaction to the testing. There should be improvement each time, because temperament testing is a form of teaching. Records should also include the pup's reaction when reintroduced to the litter. This way the breeder has an idea of each pup's personality, strengths and weaknesses. She wants to be sure they go to the right homes. She wouldn't send a shy, retiring pup into a home with a load of noisy kids and bossy parents. That would be a disaster!

Responsible breeders don't allow just anyone to adopt their dogs. They are searching for reliable, permanent homes with loving, dependable people. After advertising, they carefully screen applicants over the telephone. They ask questions: Have you ever owned a dog before? Have you owned this breed before? How long did your dog live and what did it die from? Why do you want to own this breed? What are your intentions with this dog—showing, training, family pet, breeding? Is your yard fenced and how high is the fencing? Will the dog be part of the family and live indoors? Has everyone in the family agreed about acquiring this dog? And many other possible questions.

Most callers don't pass the phone interview. The few who do are invited to see the pups. The whole family must come. The breeder wants to meet all the people who'll be living with the dog. Before they see the litter, another interview is conducted with the family to determine whether they qualify as good enough to give a home to a puppy. The breeder looks for parental control of the children. Is there any? Is it effective? Is it harsh? How do family members interact? etc.

The majority of families don't pass this part of the screening. Those who do are allowed to see only those puppies the breeder feels would best fit in with their life style. How they react in this phase of the interview determines if they pass all the tests. The responsible breeder matches a puppy to the needs of the family. She isn't just looking for homes, she's looking for *good* homes. It can take a long time to find the right home for every puppy. She may end up caring for several larger, older dogs.

A responsible breeder always offers a 30-day, money-back, no-questions-asked guarantee. She insists the new owners promise to spay/neuter the dog as soon as it is old enough. She follows up by checking back with them to be sure they have carried through on their promise. Usually, she will not release the registration papers until they supply proof of the surgery.

If they can no longer keep the animal they must return the dog to her. They must never take the dog to an animal shelter, attempt to find another home or abandon their pet. The dog must be brought back to the breeder. No responsible breeder wants any puppy she brought into the world to end up euthanized in an animal shelter, sold to a laboratory, put into a home she didn't approve of, "dumped" or abandoned.

Most responsible dog breeders don't make money breeding dogs. They invest so much time, care and money into the infrequent breedings that they're thrilled beyond words if they can break even on a litter. Their income is usually derived from a full time outside job, or a boarding, grooming, training, or pet supply business. Anyone who is not willing to do all that comprises responsible breeding becomes part of the problem of millions of animals needlessly dying yearly.

Think back to where and when you obtained Sebastian. Did you receive a 30-day guarantee? Did you promise to return him to the breeder if you could not keep him? Were you interviewed on the phone? Did your whole family have to go to choose the dog? Just because a breeder has a lot of dogs, dog kennels, ribbons, champions, etc., does not mean she is a responsible, professional breeder.

The Man-Made Dog!

Mother Nature probably created canines as animals that pair bond for life—one male and one female. The wild male wolf is not sexually mature until at least three years of age and his sperm count is high enough for procreation only in February. The wild female wolf doesn't have her first heat until she's two to three years old, and she has only one heat cycle a year, in the month of February. Only during this time does she have any sexual urges. If during her cycle she were like humans and said, "NOT THIS YEAR HONEY—I'VE GOT A HEADACHE!" there would be no wolves.

When man domesticated canines he had to use sexually aberrant animals in order to start breeding them to suit his needs. Unfortunately, domestic female dogs now have two to three estrus periods a year, usually beginning by six months of age, and domestic males are sexually mature at about six months. The sex drive is a powerful force, and intact dogs have no control over these strong biological urges.

Don't confuse your sexuality with your dog's. For humans this is a very personal issue. People have many mental sexual fantasies. Dogs don't fantasize about sex. A male dog doesn't think of ways to court a female in heat. He doesn't take her out on the town to visit fire hydrants of great renown or to the back door of a favorite restaurant, then do a bit of cat chasing to impress her. He doesn't need to prove he's a super "stud" then lie back and ask the all-important "was that as good for you as it was for me?"

A female dog doesn't grow up thinking, "When I'm old enough to have babies I'll be a great mother. I won't do the things to my puppies my mom did to me. I can hardly wait for the patter of little paws. My biological clock is ticking and I won't be totally fulfilled unless I experience the joys of motherhood!"

A dog's sexual behavior is purely biological. It's probably more realistic to say dogs don't mate for pleasure. They're biologically driven to satisfy their urges. If left unaltered, they have no choice but to satisfy their needs.

If you've ever observed dogs mating, you know there's nothing pretty about it. The female shoves her behind into the face of the male, with her tail off to one side. If he's inexperienced he mounts her leg, her face or her side. When he gets it right they go into a tie. Her sphincter muscles tighten around his penis and they rotate so they're butt to butt looking like a dog with a head at both ends. They're stuck in this position until she releases him. When released he runs off with no concern about whether she enjoyed it, is pregnant, will be a good mother to his kids or has a good home. He's only interested in finding his way home or another conquest.

The intact male dog is sexually frustrated 24 hours a day, seven days a week, 365 days a year. He can smell a female in heat for at least a one-mile and possibly a five-mile radius. He probably smells one every day of the year within that large a territory. While you're saying, "Phydeau, sit!" he may be thinking "Yeah, sure! Sit! Are you crazy? I've gotta get out of here and satisfy these urges! And you want me to sit?" The same is probably true of the female if she's in heat. She's as anxious to be with the male as he is to be with her.

To Breed or Not to Breed? ─────────────

Leaving a family pet intact is very unkind. Spaying and neutering are simple, safe procedures with many benefits. Neutering a male involves anesthetizing the dog, making a small incision in the scrotum and removing the testicles. Only a few stitches are usually required. For the females the operation is an ovariohysterectomy. The dog is anesthetized, an abdominal incision is made and the ovaries and uterus are removed. Suturing is always required.

Both operations can be performed by your personal veterinarian or at a *reputable* spay/neuter clinic. If choosing a clinic, be sure to ask if you can observe surgery there before you make an appointment. You need to know that they perform sterile surgeries where the veterinarian is capped, gowned, masked, and uses fresh sterile gloves and a fresh sterile pack for each animal. Check out the pre-op and post-op care given by the animal health technician and the volunteers. If anything appears odd, or less than sterile and humane, ask questions. If the answers aren't to your liking, look elsewhere for a more satisfactory clinic. There are some very reputable clinics operated by humane societies but there's no substitute for a personal recommendation or visit.

There are many advantages to spaying/neutering. There's no scientific evidence that a female is a healthier dog if she experiences a first heat or has one litter. Quite the opposite is true. A female spayed before her first heat cycle (four to six months of age) has very little chance of developing mammary cancers. These cancers are very common in unspayed females and undetected can lead to death. She doesn't experience the heat period with its bloody discharge. You're not visited by all the loose males in the neighborhood. There's no possibility of ovarian or uterine cancers, all the potential medical problems associated with the estrus cycle, pregnancy and birth are eliminated, and she has less chance of vaginal and anal infections. Behaviorially, she's not anxious to escape as most females in heat are, and because she's not sexually frustrated and doesn't have puppies to protect, she's less apt to become aggressive.

Medical and behavioral benefits also exist for neutered males. Behaviorally, they don't become escape artists. Most stray dogs are males who have escaped to find the females they smell. Dogs can mutilate themselves in attempts to jump, dig or chew out. Neutering at four to six months decreases aggression toward other males, and usually eliminates territorial marking behavior in the home and the disturbing habit of mounting people's legs and arms. Health benefits for the male are zero chances of testicular cancer; reduced chances for prostatic disease and cancer; conditions associated with the presence of testosterone, such as perianal tumors and perineal hernias, are less likely; and fewer penile and anal infections.

Most communities offer greatly reduced rates for

licensing altered dogs. The money you save by the reduced rates for licenses easily offsets the cost of spaying and neutering in just a few short years! Dog licensing is very important and all pet people should do it. The fees collected for licenses help to offset the costs of animal control and care of the stray animals. A licensed lost pet has a better chance of being treated medically if necessary and being reunited with his family.

Altered animals are easier to teach because they are not distracted by the urge to satisfy a physical need. I believe spaying and neutering is worth about 60 hours of teaching that you do not have to do!

Altered animals are also better watchdogs because they are not preoccupied with thoughts of escaping and mating, but rather focus their attention on the home and family. I used to have two intact males (both of whom developed testicular cancer). When the front door was opened just a crack, they were gone like a shot. Both of them were very well behaved, but when they got out that front door they were gone. We had to dash into the car and chase them down. They had one thing on their minds, and it definitely wasn't obeying commands or protecting the house!

Now I live with two neutered male dogs. When the front door is opened they run around the yard, do some sniffing and come right back when called. If someone is at the door, they just stay right there and won't let the person enter unless I approve. Both my husband and I agree, we'll never live with an intact dog again. Spayed and neutered pets live longer than the average unaltered pet, and the difference in teaching and living with them is like night and day.

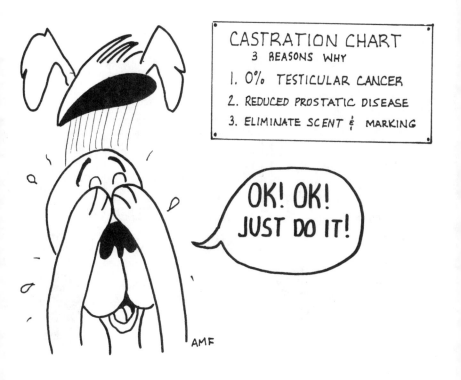

Teaching Puppies and Dogs

DON'T SEND YOUR DOG TO A TRAINER

All puppies need to be taught how to live with their human families. Many people don't think about this *before* they get the dog and then find they "don't have the time (or the desire) to train him." Some people decide to send the dog away for training and hope to get back a perfectly behaved pet. On the surface this may appear to be the solution but, in the long run, it is not.

What kind of treatment does the dog receive? What training methods are used? This kind of training is very, very expensive and usually not very long lasting. When the dog comes home he may be an angel at first but his behavior will slowly slip back to what it was before if the family has not learned to understand the dog's training. He will respond to familiar signals that caused the undesirable behavior in the first place.

Professional trainers can usually get any dog to obey them—watch a trainer take the most difficult dog in class and get him to do what the owner cannot. The important thing is not that a dog obeys a trainer but that he obeys the people he lives with. The family needs to be "trained" too!

In a good class, the instructor doesn't actually teach the puppy—she really instructs you to be your dog's teacher. This is most important because Sebastian learns from everything you do. When things are done right, he learns what you want to teach him, not some misinterpretation of what you thought you were teaching. In class, the whole family should learn how to teach the dog and thus form a close bond with Sebastian that cannot be broken. Bonding is something that never takes place when a dog is sent away for training.

KINDERGARTEN PUPPY TEACHING (KPT)

In Clarence Pfaffenberger's *The New Knowledge of Dog Behavior*, he talks about the fact that in the 1940s, out of 109 dogs in training to be Seeing Eye dogs, only nine dogs qualified at the end of training. Now that they temperament test puppies, and temperament tests are actually a form of training, 90-95% of the puppies they produce qualify. These are rather impressive statistics about the value of socializing and educating at an early age.

There are so many benefits to attending Kindergarten Puppy Teaching (KPT) classes. Anyone who doesn't take advantage of this worthwhile opportunity is really losing out! KPT is one of the best ways for Sebastian to have positive experiences and socialize with people and other dogs. He becomes confident while learning about the world he lives in. This really cannot be accomplished just by having people visit your home, taking your dog for walks, having a friend bring her dog over to your house, and certainly not by isolating Sebastian from the world.

Besides, KPT is an awful lot of fun for the puppies and their human families. It's totally impossible not to laugh or at least crack a smile while watching adorable puppies romp and play.

KPT is *definitely more important* than obedience training for a family dog. These classes are usually for puppies between the ages of seven weeks to four months. That is the socialization stage—a crucial time in Sebastian's life. Everything that happens, or doesn't happen, during this period sets up the patterns for his life. A KPT class should be limited in size, conducted in a safe, enclosed area and the instructor should ask for written proof of the puppy's shot record.

In obedience classes, trainers usually insist that only one family member do the training. I remember one case of a couple who took their dog to obedience classes. The trainer told them the wife was not to walk the dog or use any commands—the husband was the trainer and if she tried to be involved, the dog would be confused by too many masters. Three years later, the dog was biting the wife and ignoring her commands. The husband was the only one who could control him. When he had to leave on a business trip, she was bitten three times in two days while trying to feed the dog. This was certainly not a "family pet."

Since Sebastian is going to live with the family, everyone should know how to make him respond. Adopting Sebastian should have been an unanimous, family decision. No puppy should ever be obtained on impulse or "for the kids." It's a very rare child who will clean up after, instruct, feed and groom a pet. After all, most of them can't even do these things for themselves!

In KPT classes, the entire family should be involved in the teaching. The families teach their puppies without using force, intimidation or harsh methods. When Sebastian wants something (a toy, a pat, his meal, etc.), he must first say "please" by doing something that is asked of him. It's important for him to learn that his position in the family is ranked beneath all human members. This is accomplished playfully and subtly by using the command words. Then he knows how to behave, does as he is told and looks to his people for leadership.

The family is taught the methods of kindness teaching and to use the same words to mean the same things. Sebastian is sure to become confused if family members are inconsistent. A confused dog is set up to misbehave. For example, when he jumps up, if one family member says "Get down!" and another says "Get off!" and they both say "Down!" to mean the position of flattened out on the floor, this may confuse Sebastian. After all, he cannot go to the dictionary, look up "down," and learn that it means a reclined position as well as the opposite of up. The poor animal will appear to be ignoring his commands, when actually he's just confused! Consistency is the name of the game when you are teaching your dog.

In KPT classes puppies are taught the meaning of the words **Sit, Down, Come, Stay, Walk,** and **Off** using only positive reinforcement—*no* choke chains, leashes, collars or punishments. Dogs do eventually understand words and hand signals that consistently coincide with what they are being taught: **Sit, Down, Off, Ball, Toy,** etc. The puppies should be off-leash and socializing with the other puppies and people.

Two of the most important benefits of KPT classes are they learn command words and are properly socialized. Lots of puppies are scared on the first night and hide under the desk or chair. They're never forced to come out. Since they are obviously frightened, being forced to join the play group might be perceived as punishment to the puppy. By the second or third class, however, curiosity takes over and they're greeting people and playing. It's very rewarding to see a shy, fearful puppy develop into a sophisticated pet who is unafraid of new experiences.

Developing this sophistication and confidence helps to create a super family pet who will neither bite out of aggression or fear nor be fearful when presented with unknown situations. For him, new is fun, not scary. He's been taught how to learn and that learning is fun! Sebastian becomes a dog who learns new things all of his life, proving that you can "teach an old dog new tricks"!

POSITIVE REINFORCEMENT

The method of teaching discussed in this book is positive reinforcement. To paraphrase Karen Pryor in *Don't Shoot The Dog*, positive reinforcement is any act occurring in conjunction with a first act that increases the probability that the first act will be repeated.

For example, if a child walked into the room while you were having a conversation with a friend and politely tapped your shoulder to get attention, that might be a behavior you would like her to repeat, so it would be worth your while to acknowledge her and ask what she wants. You would be teaching her that behaving politely is a good way to get the reward of your attention.

On the other hand, if you were to ignore her, she would be forced to whine or otherwise misbehave until you finally shouted "*What do you want?!?*" You would be reinforcing a bad behavior and teaching her that the way to get your attention is by misbehaving.

This is also true for our spouses, our associates, our friends and our pets. The above example shows that any kind of reinforcement can cause behaviors to re-occur. If the only time you pay attention to your pet is when he's wrong, then you're teaching him to misbehave in order to get your attention.

For example, if Sebastian were in the yard barking, you'd probably open the door and bark "*Sebastian! Be quiet!*", then go inside when he was quiet. If he barked again you'd probably do the same thing in the belief that you were teaching him to stop barking.

Positive Reinforcement ─────────────

But from the dog's point of view he might have been taught the exact opposite. He was probably barking because he was lonely and bored. Like humans, the sound of his own voice lets him know that he's alive. When he barked, you rewarded him with your attention by coming to the door and saying the one word he understands—his name. He became quiet because he knew you were talking to him, but he probably didn't understand the rest of your words because *you* never took the time to teach him what they mean. When he was quiet, behaving the way you wanted, you punished him by leaving him alone again. So although your point of view was that you were trying to teach him to be quiet, you might actually have been teaching him to bark to get your attention.

On the other hand, paying more attention to Sebastian when he behaves the way you like teaches him that good behavior is rewarded by your attention. (Of course, this is much easier to do when your dog lives in the home with the family.) Therefore, if you paid a lot of attention to Sebastian when he was not barking, you'd be helping him to know that being quiet gets your attention. After all, in the course of a 24-hour day, he spends more time being quiet than he does barking.

The timing of punishments must be *very close* to the behavior being corrected, within 1.6 seconds of the occurrence. Since dogs do not have a spoken language there is no way to communicate in the past tense. The dog lives in the here and now. If he is being punished, it is because of what is happening at that precise moment. All of your words are just BLAH! BLAH! BLAH! If he is being praised, it is also because of what he is doing at that precise moment. Since reward does not have to be so precisely timed, it is not only a more effective tool but an easier tool for teaching.

The positive reinforcement method of teaching is

actually quicker than traditional dog training methods and more fun for both you and your pet. If a technique is not working, that *does not* mean something is wrong with Sebastian—you just have to modify the technique until you find something that works.

Modifying the technique may involve something called *shaping.* This entails being aware of any small step in the right direction that approximates the behavior and enlarging upon that very slowly until finally the desired behavior is accomplished. It is

45

important to always have Sebastian do a little bit more each time before he is praised or rewarded, but never to push too far too fast.

An example of shaping behavior is one I use in my classes. Since I do not believe in punishment but rather instructive reprimands, I have my students "growl" when their puppy is doing something wrong in order to startle him so he will stop the behavior and either be praised for stopping or told what to do.

Much to my surprise, "growling" does not come as naturally to everyone as it does to me! When I encounter a student who has difficulty making this noise, I have them stay after class for a "growling lesson."

We start with my demonstrating a good, loud "*AHHHHHHHH!*" and then the student tries. No matter how softly they "growl," I praise them for any noise they make, then ask them to do it again and try it with a little more force this time. If the sound is even a fraction louder, I again praise them and then ask for a little more volume on the next "growl."

Each time they try and succeed, I praise them and tell them how wonderful they are. Very quickly, they are growling almost as loudly as I can and having a grand time doing it because I am praising, encouraging, smiling and hugging. I use positive reinforcement and shaping on all of my students—four-legged and two-legged alike.

FOOD REWARDS

Most books on dog training say that you should never use food reward—I say "baloney" to that! Food reward is a wonderful teaching tool when properly used. It's more fun than using leashes, choke chains, pinch collars, punishments and other devices of inhumane treatment created by mankind. Properly used, food works wonders. The dog does what he's told not because he's afraid of failure but because you've taught him the meaning of your words. Pain never needs to be inflicted on a dog in order to achieve a well-behaved pet!

Use a small piece of food—you're not feeding Sebastian! If the food is too large he takes time to chew on it. His attention is on the food. A tiny piece can be used as a lure and a quick reward that is instantly swallowed. He comes right back looking for more and you can continue teaching!

In the beginning, whenever you're teaching Sebastian something new, use continuous reinforcement—every time he does what you want, reward him. You're like a vending machine. With a vending machine, every time you put in money and pull the lever, you get a reward—the candy bar.

When Sebastian demonstrates that he knows what a word means, convert to intermittent reinforcement—he is randomly rewarded. You become a slot machine. With a slot machine, you put in money, pull the lever and sometimes coins come back and sometimes they don't—you never know what will happen until it happens!

It has been determined that if you continuously reinforce a behavior, it may become erratic. The dog obeys only if he is hungry and if he feels like it. If you never reinforce the behavior, it may disappear—you wouldn't sit very long at a slot machine that never spat some coins back at you! But when intermittently reinforced, the behavior stays very constant—no one leaves a slot machine that pays off now and again.

You are teaching Sebastian to do what he is told, not *because* you have food but because now he understands your words and *maybe* this time he'll be rewarded. He might think like this, "I know what that word means and sometimes she rewards me with tidbits when I do as she says. I hope this is the time she has the tidbit! I better do what she says!" Now you don't need food to have him obey. He does what you say whether or not you have a treat, because he *knows* what your words mean and *hopes* he'll get a tidbit! Anyone not using food as a teaching tool is really missing out on a super *fun* way to instruct their dog!

Food is not the only reward. You can use anything Sebastian likes or wants. When you interact with him to fulfill his doggy needs you have a teaching opportunity. At feeding times, use the whole bowl of food as a lure for a **Sit**, then as a reward. If he brings his ball to you for a game of retrieve, use the ball as a lure to **Sit**, then throw the ball as a reward. If Sebastian is standing on one side of the door and wants to get to the other side, use your hand as a lure for a **Sit**, then let him in or out as a reward.

When he nudges your elbow for a pat, if you automatically reach down and pet him, then he's teaching you! Imagine if Sebastian had some doggy friends over for a visit. He might tell them, "Watch this neat trick I taught my people. I just nudge their elbow and they automatically reach down to pet me!" When Sebastian nudges you for a pat, tell him to **Sit**, then pet him briefly as a reward. You've taken control of the situation. The dog obeys the words because you taught him their meaning and praised the behaviors, not because of a leash or choke chain.

Another major benefit of using food rewards is that you're teaching hand signals and words at the very same time. The way your hand moves while luring the dog into a position becomes a hand signal to Sebastian. He is more aware of body language than of spoken language and learns the hand signals much more quickly.

Once Sebastian starts to respond to your hand motions when you lure him with the food, then try saying the command word just before you make the hand motion. In this way, he will be taught that the hand signal and the spoken word have the same meaning and will soon respond to either one separately or both used together. It is beneficial to continue to use voice and hand signals together because as dogs age they can lose their sight or hearing. If Sebastian is proficient at both methods, then you can continue to communicate with him even though he may not hear or see you.

Teaching Sebastian off-leash, with food reward and hand signals, saves lots of time. Dogs are very sensitive to body language. When trained with a choke chain and leash most dogs are inadvertently taught that removal of these items signals the release from having to obey. When taught off-leash from the start, the release is either a hand signal or a spoken release word. He doesn't have to be re-taught

49

his commands just because you removed the collar or leash.

VOICE

When you use your voice as a means of teaching, requesting, commanding, demanding or reprimanding, you don't need to buy lots of "training" equipment. Your voice is all that you need and it is always with you! How the voice is used depends upon the individual, the dog, the situation, etc. For example, if you have a shy or fearful dog you certainly wouldn't want to use a bellowing roar to reprimand him. A simple AHH! would most likely suffice. An excitable and rambunctious dog would need a deep, throaty growl of an *AHHHHHHHHHH!*

It is easier if Sebastian has one word commands; each command is a different word and everyone in the family uses the same word to mean the same thing. When teaching a command word such as **Sit,** as Sebastian sits, say **Sit! Good sit!** with a happy, pleased voice. The command is said this way because you're teaching the meaning of the word **Sit**. The first **sit** is called the primary command—that's the word you're teaching Sebastian. **Good** is the praise word, and the second **sit** is called the secondary reinforcer—it strengthens the sound of the word you're teaching.

Words cannot be used as commands until the dog demonstrates he understands their meaning. Periodically test his comprehension by saying the word as a command to see what he does. If he sits when you say **Sit** or downs when you say **Down** and you've tried this several times to be sure it wasn't a coincidence, then the word can be used as a command. When a word becomes a command you can expect Sebastian to do as you say.

Do *not* continuously repeat the command words. Rather, the first time say it politely Sebastian, **Sit!** If he doesn't sit within a reasonable amount of time, then

put in a verbal reprimand and command the sit—
AHHHH! **Sit!** If he still doesn't sit, then hold him by his
cheeks, look him straight in the eye (obtaining eye
contact with your dog is a very effective way of
establishing that you are the leader), growl the human
equivalent of a doggy growl and demand a sit—
AHHHHHHHHHH! Sit! That will certainly cause him to
obey. Then smile and praise him—**Good sit!**

Once he knows the meaning of the word, Sebastian
should never receive a food treat or reward if you have to
say the command more than once. You want to teach
Sebastian that he must **Sit** when told to. If you have to go
through the routine of politely asking, then commanding
and possibly even demanding, a simple word of praise is all
that he has earned. In this manner, you will be teaching
him to obey commands that are said only once because it's
easier and more pleasant, and the rewards come only if he
obeys when politely asked!

The tone of your voice can make the difference
between a dog who works for you and one who doesn't.
If you use an angry voice all the time, Sebastian never
knows when he's done well. A monotonic voice is
boring so he will want to go off to find something more
fun to do. If your voice is joyful and exciting, he feels
jovial and wants to please you.

Your voice should also be confident. If there is doubt
in your voice when giving commands, he may try to
please you by not obeying since you really don't expect
compliance anyway! *There is a difference between a
confident voice of authority and a bossy, angry voice.* If
your tone conveys confidence, Sebastian wants to
please you by doing as you say.

Take the time to teach him what words mean not by
reprimanding for mistakes but by praising for
successes. He obeys because he *understands* what you
want. Dogs like to please. Given a fair chance to learn
words and rules, they joyously do as they're told.

TEACHING SESSIONS

In the past people have been told to work with their dog for at least 30 minutes twice a day. Who has an extra 30 minutes two times a day to work their dog? This is another bit of rubbish! Every time you do anything with Sebastian you're *teaching* him. The three easiest ways are:

1. WATCH SEBASTIAN. When he does something you'd like him to repeat, tell him what he's doing. If you're observing him and he's going into a **sit** position, say **Sit! Good sit!** as he is in the act of sitting. That is teaching!

2. MAKE EVERY INTERACTION COUNT. If he is standing by the door to go out tell him to **Sit! Good sit!** then reward him by letting him out. Make him **Sit! Good sit!** then **Stay! Good stay!** before you put his bowl of food down.

If Sebastian drops his ball by you and you automatically pick it up and throw it, then he is teaching you a command to throw the ball. That is not the way it should be! Instead, use the ball to lure him into a **Sit! Good sit!** then throw it as a reward. You are teaching your dog a polite way to ask for what he wants and to look to you for fair leadership! You have to interact with him every day—feeding him, letting him in and out, playing with him, petting him, etc.—make him say, "Please and thank you!" by doing a simple **Sit! Good sit!** for you first!

3. TEACHING SESSIONS. These should last no more than five minutes at a time, as many times a day as you want. For example, you can teach during television commercials, between household chores, while waiting

for food to zap in the microwave, etc.

Don't repeat the same thing over and over again—that's boring for you and Sebastian. If you want to teach **Sit** and he does a **sit,** you've been successful—*quit!* If you want to spend more time with him, try **Walk, Down** or **Stay.** Try to end the session with Sebastian being successful. Don't continue working until he is a failure. Instead, let the last image of playing these learning games always be success. Then you can both look forward to the next interaction.

When a teaching session goes very badly—you cannot get Sebastian to do anything and you're feeling quite angry—*quit!* He's not getting away with disobeying. Since he didn't **sit,** you didn't say anything! He received no praise or reward. The whole episode was nothing more than a non-productive interaction between you and Sebastian. Try again later when you've calmed down. If you're not having fun, then neither is Sebastian. He's very aware of your mood and responds accordingly.

If you've had a lousy day at work or the freeway traffic was unbearable and all you really want to do is get home and forget the world—don't teach Sebastian that day. A whole day without teaching will not cause any catastrophes—no one will repossess your car, foreclose on your house, or fire you from your job because you didn't teach your dog.

Sometimes dogs seem to hit a learning plateau. After several weeks of learning and making you proud Sebastian may experience an overload of brain circuits and will not even do a simple **sit.** He is not acting ornery—he just needs some time off and some simple reminders.

Anytime you encounter a problem with something he already knows—always back up. Ease off the teaching during this time and go back to basics. Reteach the **Sit** as if he had never learned it. By backing off and giving

him time to straighten out the circuits, you'll find that in a week or so Sebastian is performing better than before and ready to learn more new things!

If it takes a little longer, so what? Who cares? You have a good 10 to 15 years with Sebastian. Put everything into its proper perspective—you're only trying to teach the family dog! Sometimes a day off from teaching can work wonders—it keeps you both from getting bored and you'll be surprised at how excited Sebastian will be the next day about your special time together. He'll work extra hard to please you! Teaching should always be *fun* for both of you. Relax, enjoy each other and make teaching time your *fun* time together.

OFF

Off is one of the most useful, effective words to teach Sebastian. It means whatever he is touching, with whatever part of his body, don't touch it! If his front paws are on the kitchen counter, then you want his paws **off** the counter. If his teeth are on your clothes, then you want his teeth **off** your clothes. If his body is on the couch, then you want him **off** the couch. If he's jumping on you, then you want him **off** you. This is such a great command!

Sebastian should not put his mouth on your hands while you're holding a food lure. You want him to be interested in the food but you don't want to be bitten while holding it. With a handful of treats, let him have one, just for free! Hold another treat in his face, if he puts his teeth on it say **Off!** If he doesn't back away, push him away forcefully, but gently, with the back of your hand under his chin and say **Off!** When he backs away, say **Good off! Take it!** and feed him the treat. Repeat the process. If he immediately backs away when you say **Off!**, then say **Good off! Take it!** and feed him the treat. If he doesn't back away, push him away as you say **Off!** Now, say **Off!** and count to three. If he doesn't touch the food, say **Good off! Take it!** and feed him. If he touches the treat before you get to three, push him away and start counting from one again. Repeat the game and gradually increase the time he must not touch the food. Wiggle the treat to tempt him. He must learn not to take food from your hand unless you say **Take it!**

When Sebastian is jumping on you say **Off!** Back away from him so he falls to the ground, say **Good off!** and pet him. If his feet are on the coffee table say **Off!** If he doesn't get off, quickly swish him off as you demand

Off! When his feet are on the floor say **Good off!** If he jumps on the door to get in or out tell him **Off!** Back away from the door and give him no attention until he stops jumping at the door. Tell him **Good off!**, pet him and let him in or out.

The nice thing about **Off** is you can growl it at the dog to let him know that he is displeasing you. When Sebastian stops the undesirable behavior, smile with your face and voice as you say **Good off!** Most people pay attention to the dog only when he is doing something unacceptable. He soon learns to do those things to get attention.

I remember one student who just could not accept saying **Good off!** when her dog stopped jumping on her. She was sure he would think she was praising the jumping. I explained that 1.6 seconds after an event is too late for punishment but she could not accept that. She wanted to treat the dog the same as her children. She was convinced if they received praise for stopping misbehaviors they would be incorrigible little monsters. I asked her to bring the children to the next session.

She was absolutely right—they were incorrigible little monsters! She spent the entire time yelling and reprimanding. They paid no attention to her. All that screaming was just noise to them.

They were into everything. No matter how much she tried to handle the situation, it was out of control. I told the kids the next time they opened a cupboard door they would hear a blood curdling **Off!** from me. That meant they had better close the door and leave it alone or they would have to leave. One tested me. I screamed **"O-O-O-F-F-F-F-F!"** so loudly that I swear even the clock stopped running! She stopped what she was doing; I very kindly thanked her for stopping and gave her a lifesaver! She was so stunned, she went to the cupboard, closed it and then sat down very quietly. Her mother never said a word!

While they were at my puppy school, her dog put his paws on my desk. I growled **Off!** just once. When he stopped, I said **Good off!,** gave him a liver treat and made a great fuss over him. The entire time he was at the center he never again put his paws on the desk.

A dog cannot read a psychology book to learn about negative and positive attention. If you never say **Good off!,** for example, he learns to be a "brat" and jump just to hear you growl **Off!** To him any attention is better than being ignored. Always yelling at Sebastian and never praising him teaches him to "misbehave" to be noticed. It is very important to praise him when he does something right.

SIT

To teach the meaning of **Sit,** first define it! **Sit** means put your rear end on the floor. It's something all dogs do naturally. You don't have to push on Sebastian's behind for him to do it. One way to teach him is to watch him. Every time you see him *in the act of* putting his tush on the floor say **Sit! Good sit!** If every time he puts his rear on the floor, you tell him what he's doing, he will soon "understand" what **sit** means. After all, word association with what's happening at the time is the same way you were taught language.

Another way to teach **sit** is to lure Sebastian into a **sit** position. Hold a tidbit on Sebastian's nose and slowly move your hand up and back, keeping the food on his nose. If you hold it too high he will jump. As his head moves up and back, his behind naturally goes down. When his tush goes for the floor say **Sit! Good sit!** and give him the reward.

Sometimes, especially with older puppies and dogs, as the food moves back the dog just backs up. If this happens, back Sebastian into a corner. As you lure his head up and back, he has to **sit** because there is no space to back up. Another way would be to *gently* hold onto the buckle collar under his chin as you lure his head up and back. Do *not* use the collar to make him **sit**—use it only to prevent him from backing up.

If none of these methods works, you may have to do some shaping. Reward Sebastian for any small step that is involved in a **sit.** First reward the head going up; say **Sit! Good sit!** with little enthusiasm and feed him a small treat. Now, lure the head up and back a little before you say **Sit! Good sit!** again with no excitement and feed him the treat. Next, the head is lured up and back and the back end scrunches a little. Say **Sit! Good sit!** with a little happiness and feed him the tidbit. Now he must get his head up and back, his back end must scrunch a little and his hind legs must fold a little bit. Say **Sit! Good sit!** with a bit of animation and give him the treat.

Finally, lure his head up and back; the back end scrunches, the legs fold and the tush is on the floor. This time say **SIT! GOOD SIT!** with great joy and enthusiasm and give him all the treats in your hand. Don't try another **sit** right away. Let the last image on Sebastian's brain be success, your smiling face and happy voice, and the memory of that humungous food reward! You may have to repeat this sequence a few times. Before long Sebastian is sitting when he sees your hand moving up and back.

Next, you must be able to attach a leash to his collar without him jumping or struggling. To accomplish this, accustom him to the sequence of sitting, touching his collar, then being praised. Say **Sit,** touch his collar with your hand, say **Good sit!** and then give the reward. He learns to enjoy having his collar touched because he associates it with receiving praise and reward.

Remember, when teaching Sebastian to do anything new, always reward each success. Don't keep repeating the exercise. If he does one good **sit,** don't make him **sit** again and again. That's very boring! You're setting him up for a failure. It's best to quit after a successful effort. Let the last image of playing the **sit** game be that he succeeded and got a reward for the behavior, and that you were very happy. Both of you can look forward to playing the **sit** game again.

COME

Most people don't really think about what **come** is like from the dog's point of view. Therefore, the three basic rules of **come** must be discussed before defining the word:

RULE 1: *Never* punish the dog when he comes to you. There is obvious punishment such as: "Sebastian, **Come!** You *bad* dog, look what you did! *Bad, bad, bad!*" And there is not-so-obvious punishment, unless you see things from the dog's point of view: The dog is indoors with the family, having a good time, and for some reason you want to put him outside—"Sebastian, **Come!** Outside you go!" Sebastian might perceive having to go outside and being isolated from the family as a punishment. Since the last thing Sebastian did before this punishment happened was **come** to you, he may interpret this as a punishment for **coming**. Therefore, before you **come** your dog always ask yourself these three questions:

1. Why am I calling Sebastian?

2. What do I intend to do with Sebastian when he gets here?

3. Could Sebastian even remotely conceive of this as a negative happening?

If the answer to question three is even a vague "Gee, I don't know, maybe!" then don't **come** him—go and get him instead.

In the above example, instead of calling Sebastian to **come** to you so you can put him outside, *go to* Sebastian. Play with him a second or two, tell him **walk,** then walk him to the door and outside. Go outside and play with him a couple of minutes before you leave him alone. You accomplish the same goal of having the dog outside, but without any negative association with a **come.**

Come

RULE 2: Your dog's name should never be used as a command. People very often shout the dog's name in an angry voice when he is "naughty" and expect him to stop what he's doing. They also shout the dog's name and expect the dog to come running. You've heard it many times. The neighbor's dog is loose and she's going up and down the street shouting, "Phydeau! Phydeau! Phydeau!" But she never tells Phydeau what she wants him to do!

If someone shouted your name, you probably wouldn't go running to them. In all likelihood, you would look in their direction and say something like, "Yeah! What do you want?" The same is true for the dog. Your dog's name, just like your name, is an attention- getting device. Names are used to speak to a specific dog (or person), or get his attention so you can tell him what you want.

Therefore, the command should not be **Come,** Sebastian. The dog may not pay attention until he hears his name. Since the command preceded his name he probably missed it. He may turn around and look at you as if to say "What do you want?" But you think he is disobeying by not **coming** right away. The command should always be Sebastian, **Come!** Be sure you have the dog's attention before you tell him what to do!

RULE 3: Never give the **Come** command and let the dog get away without **coming.** Every time you let this happen, you are informing Sebastian that **come** is not really that important, and if he chooses not to do it that's all right with you. If you just keep saying **Come! Come! Come!. . . . ,** Sebastian doesn't come and you just give up, then **come** is just a noise that you have taught him to ignore. Anytime you say **Come** be sure you make it happen. Don't carelessly throw this word about.

Everyone wants the dog to **come** when called. But **come** may not be the wisest command to use if, for some reason, you have allowed Sebastian to be off-leash in an unfenced area and he runs away. For example, if he has managed to navigate across the street and you **come** him, he has to cross the street again—double jeopardy! The smart way would be to command Sebastian to **Sit** and **Stay,** then *you* cross the street and go to him.

Now, let's define **come.** It simply means move towards me. Anytime your dog moves toward you he is doing a **come.** Since it is an act all dogs do, you don't have to teach them how to **come**—you just have to teach the meaning of the word. Sebastian must learn that coming to you always makes you happy and is a positive experience for him.

Most people want to place the dog in a stay, walk away from him, then say **Come.** The problem with this method is that humans are creatures of habit and not often aware of the habit. The amount of time that elapses between the command **Stay** and the command **Come** is always about the same, give or take a couple of seconds. This consistency teaches the dog to hold the **stay** for just so long, then start to move toward you—after all, the reward is always given when he gets to you. He never receives praise for **stay** but always gets attention when he moves to you. If you intend to try a long **stay** and go back to Sebastian, after the usual time lapse he thinks you made a mistake and forgot to say **Come.** Since he wants to please you, he **comes** even though he wasn't called. Many dogs break the **stay** because of being taught **come** in this manner.

There are better ways than using **stay.** Remember, **come** just means move towards me—nothing very fancy. When you are alone with Sebastian, go up to him with a treat in your hand, a smile on your face and great joy in your voice. Waggle the tidbit in his face and talk sweetly to him. Now start to back up as you hold the lure in front of you. He should follow the tidbit. If you're backing up, then the dog is *moving toward you.*

Come

Say Sebastian, **Come! Good come! Good come! Good come!. . . . . . .** and give him the treat.

Anytime Sebastian is moving toward you, say Sebastian, **Come! Good come! Good come!. . . .** You tell him what he is doing when he is doing it. Notice the command, Sebastian, **Come!** is said just once, then the praise **Good come! Good come!. . .** is repeated several times to encourage him to continue moving toward you. He must learn to **Come** on one command: Sebastian, **Come!** not Sebastian, **Come! Come! SEBASTIAN, COME!**

Another method requires the assistance of at least one other person. Person A restrains Sebastian until Person B actually says Sebastian, **Come!** Person B comes up to the dog with a big smile on the face and in the voice, presents the tidbit and says some really sweet nothings such as, "Hi, Sebastian! What a good dog you are! You are so pretty! What a lovely boy!" etc.

This gets his attention focused on the person holding the lure, not the one holding him. Then Person B runs away. Sebastian's instinct is to chase after something that runs away from him. Now, Person B squats down. When standing upright, people appear very tall and large—a possible threat—and Sebastian cannot see the face clearly when he gets too close. It is very important for a dog to be able to see your face in order to know how you are feeling about him. By squatting, the person appears smaller and more playful, and Sebastian can **come** in all the way and still see that smiling, joyous, loving face!

Now the person who ran away calls the dog: Sebastian, **Come! Good come! Good come!. . .** As he **comes** in close, she feeds him the tidbit and says **Good come!** Do *not* reach out and grab him—that is a very threatening gesture! If you insistently reach over his head to grab or pet him, you may create a dog who will never **come** in nice and close because he doesn't like

what happens when he gets there. Instead, feed him
the treat and give him a quick chuck under the chin or
on the chest! Touching under the chin or on the chest
is very friendly and will help to convince Sebastian that
coming is fun and **coming** in close is nothing to fear.

If Sebastian does not **come** when you try this game,
you may have run too far away. In the beginning,
especially with small dogs and puppies, it is better to
run only a couple of steps away and gradually increase
the distance until Sebastian **comes** no matter how far
away you are.

When you begin teaching **come,** always set
Sebastian up to succeed. During the first week, don't
even use the word **come** except when you are playing
the teaching games described above. Teach **come** when
he is not distracted with something else. Add
distractions *after* you have taught him what **come**
means and what it feels like to succeed *every* time he
hears the word.

Once he knows the word, then it is essential that you
call him when he is busy! Try calling him when he is
eating a snack or meal, chewing on his toy, playing
with another dog, playing with a person, etc.

If you call him when he is distracted and he does not
come, don't let him get away with it. Go to him, take
the object of distraction, waggle it in front of him as you
proceed to back up, and make him walk a few steps
toward you as you say Sebastian, **Come! Good come!
Good come!. . .** Give the object back to him and tell
him to **go play!** If he is playing with a person, or
chasing a butterfly, take a tidbit to lure him to you but
don't feed him the food every time; the reward for
coming to you is that he can go back to what he was
doing. It is always a good idea to use the distraction as
the lure and then let Sebastian have it back as the
reward for **coming!**

WALK

The definition of **Walk** is the dog **walks** nicely by your side. It's O.K. to get a little ahead or behind. Not so far ahead, however, that he's pulling you down the street, or so far behind that you're dragging him into the veterinarian's office.

Most pet people want a dog who **walks** without pulling. The reason most dogs pull on a leash is that they are inadvertently taught to. Imagine someone putting a collar around your neck, attaching a leash to it, and tugging you toward them. Your reflex is to pull away. The more they pull you to them, the more you pull away. If they persist in tugging, you soon learn to pull as soon as they attach the leash.

This is true for Sebastian, too. He is doing the best he can under the circumstances. He also has a reflex to pull in the opposite direction of the force exerted. Pulling becomes a game. When you attach a leash to his collar and pull him to you, he naturally pulls away. The more you pull, the more he pulls. Before long, you've taught him to pull on a leash.

Walk is the most difficult command to teach because none of what we want from Sebastian makes any sense from his point of view. Dogs naturally walk with their noses on the ground, sniffing trails, etc.—we want them to **walk** with their heads up high watching us. When dogs walk on their own they zig-zag along as they pursuit a specific scent—we usually walk in a straight line on the sidewalk or path. Also, the dog's instinct is to stay as far away from our feet as possible to avoid being stepped on—we want him to walk as close to us as he can get. The dog's point of view about walking and ours are miles apart, so it is up to us to make it worth Sebastian's while to do it our way because it's more fun, pleasant and rewarding for both of us!

In conventional obedience training, dogs are trained to heel on-leash, then trained to do it off-lead. That's the hard way! It is better and easier to first instruct him as to what you mean when you say **Walk,** without attaching the leash. Then, when you do attach it to his collar and say **Walk,** instead of a tug-o-war ensuing, he'll understand what you want him to do.

Practice off-leash only inside your home and fenced yard. It's very dangerous to let a dog run without a leash except in enclosed areas such as schoolyards and ballparks. Be sure to obtain permission to use such enclosures, because most communities do not allow dogs in public areas. It's also against the law in most communities for dogs to run free. No matter how well behaved Sebastian may be, he's still a dog. At any time, he may decide to chase after a cat, child, etc. Don't use the leash as a "training" tool. Teach the meaning of **walk** and use the leash as a safety device.

I'm sure you're wondering how to make Sebastian **walk** close to you without a leash when you can't do it with the leash! It's simple—use a food lure. Decide which side you want him on and always use that same side. Everyone in the family should agree on and use the same side.

Traditionally a dog is **walked** on the left. In AKC obedience, he *must* **walk** on the left. If you're more comfortable with him on the right and have no intentions of entering competitions, use the right side.

Sometimes dogs will have a side preference. If you are **walking** Sebastian on the right and he keeps trying to go to your left, try **walking** with him on your left; he may be more comfortable there. You can even allow him to pull you down the street if you both enjoy it and aren't interested in **walking** side by side. He's your dog. You can make any rules you like, as long as you're fair, consistent and humane.

After determining the side, hold a small food lure in that hand. If Sebastian **walks** on the left, the lure is in the left hand; if he's on the right, the lure is in the right hand. Wiggle the tidbit to get his attention. Then hold it directly in Sebastian's face. If you have a small dog you may have to bend over a little. If the lure is too high it causes him to jump and hop instead of **walk.**

With the food in the dog's face, take a few steps. He should follow your hand and **walk** with you. As he moves with you say **Walk!** Let him take two steps with you, then say **Good walk!** and feed him the reward. Try it again. See if he can take three steps, then five steps, then 10 steps, etc.

Another way is by *watching* the dog. When you're walking and the dog proceeds to **walk** by your side, tell him what he's doing— say **Walk! Good walk!**

When Sebastian **walks** nicely, off-lead, in the house and yard, attach a leash to his collar and let it drag while you **walk.** Pick up the leash occasionally, draping it loosely over your hand for a few steps.

Tightening or choking up on the leash is a mistake most people make, and it causes the dog to pull because he doesn't have to pay attention to you.

When Sebastian is leash-walking nicely in the house and yard, slowly stage going for a walk. You can't suddenly attempt to **walk** around the block. If he pulled you before, he will again. So far, he's been taught successful leash-walking only in the house and yard.

Now, show him that he must **walk** as you go out the gate. When he's comfortable **walking** out the gate, add five steps beyond the gate, then 10 steps, etc. If he pulls, you've progressed too quickly. Back up to the last successful location. Work a little longer on that, then progress at a slower pace.

When you can **walk** from the gate to the sidewalk, try **walking** to the next house. Add only one house at a time, then turn around and go back. Slowly teach him to **walk** around the block obeying the **Walk** command. Whenever he starts to pull, end the walk and go back home. The punishment for pulling is that the walk is over. Once he realizes his pulling signals the end of the walk, he'll refrain from pulling.

When Sebastian makes a mistake, do the opposite to accent his mistake. Most people stop if the dog lags. You should speed up. If he pulls ahead, turn around and go the other way. You're taking him for a walk, not the other way around!

Try not to use walking as a way to exercise Sebastian. Dogs love to go for walks and just hearing or seeing the leash is enough to excite most dogs. It would be dreadful to destroy that enthusiasm by making the **walk** an ordeal of punishments.

Instead, exercise Sebastian by throwing the ball or frisbee. Linda Goodman's rule of thumb for walking a dog is, "never walk a wired dog—always walk a tired dog!" Run him around the yard, put him through his paces on his commands. Then, as a reward for good behavior, take him for a short walk. Don't give the **Walk** command right away—let him have some fun at first. Then tell him to **Walk.** Because he has burned off a lot of his energy, he will be more apt to obey the **Walk** command. Gradually, you can take longer walks.

If you have a persistent puller and no method is working, you may want to try one of the new head collars. They don't choke, pinch, stick with prongs or use electric shock. Choke chains and pinch collars work on the dog's neck. Most dogs are not sensitive on the neck because there are very strong muscles in that area—if he feels it at all, it's just an annoyance. A tug-o-war will take place.

The head collars simultaneously exert pressure to the back of the head and jaws, imitating control by mother and leader dogs. Pressure on the dog's face causes him to turn his head back to see what's happening. Where his head goes, you can be sure his body will follow. You get Sebastian's attention to tell him what he should be doing.

The head collars help control behavior by demonstrating that you are the leader. Working the snout gets his attention quickly because it is a sensitive area. If I put a ring through your nose and gave a gentle tug, I bet anything you'd do whatever I wanted! So does Sebastian! Try the teaching methods outlined before using a head collar but don't hesitate to resort to

one of these humane devices if all else has failed!

Most dogs love to go for nice long walks with their owners. Walking should be fun! It's exciting and something Sebastian can really look forward to! If you're a boring grouch, he has no incentive to stay close. Be happy and joyful, and talk to him.

DOWN

Down means the act of flattening out on the floor. Don't worry about perfection—if he falls onto his side or rolls onto his back, accept those as **downs** also. **Down** is a comfortable position and can be very relaxing to a dog—they very often just fall asleep after a while. When Sebastian is in a **down** he is actually in a submissive position. Having him **stay** in a **down** position helps you to gain control and respect without intimidation.

There are several ways to make Sebastian **down.** Try them all to see which one(s) work for you. If they all work, use them all to add variety to the teaching. If only one works, then that's the one you have to use.

1. Watch the dog. Anytime you see Sebastian *in the act of* going **down** tell him what he's doing. Say **Down! Good down!** No food lure or reward is necessary. You don't even have to be near him for this method to work. Don't forget, you're not using the word as a command yet. You're just teaching him what the word means.

2. On a tile or wood floor, not a carpeted one, hold a small food lure under Sebastian's nose. Then drop your hand slowly, *straight* to the floor. Just hold the lure there and let him bite and dig at it. Once he starts to use his paws at the lure he will probably drop into a **down.** As he's going down say **Down! Good down!** and feed him the reward. This method is usually successful with young puppies.

3. Tell Sebastian to **Sit.** Using the same lure, slowly move the tidbit *straight* to the floor so his nose lands on the floor between his two front paws. Then slowly slide it away from him. He should follow the lure with his nose and just slide into a **down.** If he goes down say **Down! Good down!** and feed him the reward. If he stands up, you may not have moved the tidbit *straight*

to the floor. If the lure is moved forward too soon the dog is forced to stand to keep up with it.

If the lure is definitely going *straight* to the floor and Sebastian insists on standing, then, with him in a **sit,** *very lightly* place your hand on his withers (shoulder blades) as you slowly move the food *straight* to the floor and out. You mustn't push him into the **down.** Your hand on the withers is just to prevent him from standing up. If he starts to stand, exert only enough pressure to keep him in a **sit.** Don't push him into the **down.** Continue moving the lure to the floor and out and as he goes down say **Down! Good down!** and feed the reward. After several times with your hand *gently* on the withers, try it without touching him. Puppies catch on very quickly!

If he still does not **down,** try some shaping. Have a handful of treats and tell Sebastian to **Sit.** With your hand gently on his withers, use a tidbit to lure his head straight to the floor, place the tidbit there for him and say **Down! Good down!** While he is eating that reward, place another one an inch or two further out and tap your finger at the lure to get his attention. As he stretches his head further to get the tidbit say **Down! Good down!** As he is eating, place another one further out and keep repeating this until he finally lies **down.** When he accomplishes this great feat, give him all the treats in your hand, say **Down! Good down!** with great joy and give him lots of love and kisses.

4. Another way to get Sebastian **down** is for you to sit on the floor with your legs spread apart. Make a bridge with one of your legs by bending it at the knee while your foot is flat on the floor. Hold the lure under the knee and wiggle it around to get his attention. Slowly slide the tidbit beneath your knee, luring Sebastian to crawl under. As he crawls along he has to go into a **down.** Say **Down! Good down!** and feed him the reward. This method is almost foolproof and lots of

fun, especially for young children.

If you have trouble with this method, some shaping may be necessary. With one hand full of treats, lure Sebastian to the "bridge" and place a treat right under your knee. Say **Down! Good down!** as he takes the treat and immediately place another one a little further along while he is still eating. Tap at the new treat to get his attention and as he moves along to get it say **Down! Good down!** Now place another treat further along and keep repeating this until Sebastian is flat on the floor. At this point, say **Down! Good down!** with lots of enthusiasm and give him all the treats in your hand and a great big hug!

STAY

Stay is an important command. **Stay** means I am going to move away from you, don't leave that spot until I come back and release you. (Don't do out of sight **stays**. As long as the dog can see you, he must hold the **stay**.)

Unlike obedience-oriented people, if the dog is told to **Sit** then **Stay** and lies **down,** he is not to be reprimanded. Obedience people say the dog has disobeyed the last command by changing position. Pet people know the last command was **Stay,** not **Sit!** If the dog lies **down** but doesn't leave his location, he is still in a **stay!**

When teaching the **Stay** command, be sure Sebastian is either in a **Sit** or **Down.** If the dog is standing he can easily just walk away. But in a **Sit** or **Down** he has to change position before he can move. That gives you the time to correct him. Also, do not use the dog's name when saying **Stay.** Hearing his name implies to him that an action is going to follow, but **stay** is a non-action command.

The hand signal for **stay** is a flick of the wrist with a flat palm in front of Sebastian's face. Do *not* pop him on the nose. That's annoying, unnecessary and no fun for him. Be sure there is no food in the signal hand. If you flash food in his face, then step away, Sebastian is being set up to fail. He wants to follow the scent of the lure and break the **Stay.** Good teaching takes advantage of successes. When the dog succeeds and receives praise he is more likely to repeat the successful behavior.

With your right hand full of tidbits, stand in front of Sebastian, tell him to **Sit** or **Down,** give the **stay** signal with your left hand and say **Stay.** Step back on your right foot, don't move your left foot at all. Then, *immediately* step forward on your right foot and reach forward with your right hand to feed a food reward as you say **Good stay!**

If you're standing in front of Sebastian and he moves with you each time, try standing beside him. With him at your left side and both of your feet together, give the **stay** signal with your left hand as you say **Stay,** move your right foot one step to the right, then bring it back so both feet are together again. Reach across your body with your right hand and say **Good stay** as you feed him the reward.

I usually recommend that owners get the rhythm of these movements by practicing in front of a mirror before they try it with the dog. When you've got it down pat, you will be able to say **Stay,** move away, come back and say **Good stay** so quickly it seems as if it all happens at once!

If you do the steps correctly, your left foot does not actually move away from the dog but your body gives the illusion of having moved away. In the beginning, all that is really necessary is this illusion because you are teaching the meaning of a new word.

Don't wait to see if he will **stay**—he will not. If you move too slowly the dog will move and fail. You must get back to the dog before he has a chance to move. It is essential that you move away and return quickly because Sebastian must not be set up to fail. The object is to get back to him before he has a chance to move so he can be praised for a successful **stay.**

At first Sebastian may think

you're nuts! He does nothing, you feed him and tell him **Good.** But that is exactly what **stay** means— don't move from where you are until I return and let you go. Do about four or five very quick **stays,** then try one where you actually move *both* feet just one step away from the dog and go right back. If he breaks the **stay,** give a quick verbal reprimand, make him complete one of the very rapid **stays** and let him go.

Anytime he fails, verbally reprimand him, then make him do one quick **stay** before you quit. The last image on his brain from playing the **Stay** game should be that he succeeded. That way, next time you play the game, he is reminded of the success and praise rather than failure and a reprimand.

SEBASTIAN, COME !

Gradually increase the amount of time Sebastian must hold the **Stay** with you just one step away from him. Try five seconds, seven seconds, 10 seconds, 12 seconds, etc. If he does well at five seconds and seven seconds, but fails when you try 10 seconds, reprimand him verbally (AHHHHHH!), get him back to a **Sit** or **Down,** do a very quick **stay,** praise him, reward him and end the game. About an hour later try again. Start with a quick one, then a seven second **stay,**

AMF

then an eight second **stay,** then nine seconds and so forth. Your goal is to gradually build the **Stay** time to 30 seconds. When he holds a 30 second **stay,** then you can start to add distance. Thirty seconds may not sound like a long time, but try holding your breath or waiting for a microwave for 30 seconds!

You are still only one step away from Sebastian while increasing the time. The reason for this is twofold:

1. The further away you are from him, the less control you have and he is aware of that. He knows if you can't reach him, you can't stop him from moving.

2. It takes time to add distance. You have to be able to walk away and then walk back to him.

When you increase the distance, do it one step at a time, as gradually and methodically as you added time. Do two steps, then three steps, etc. When you go further than Sebastian can tolerate and he breaks the **Stay,** verbally reprimand him, do a quick half-step **stay** and end the game. In about an hour try again. When you reach the distance of the last failure, try adding only half a step at a time, until he can **stay** no matter where you are in the room.

Now, add distractions in the room to tempt Sebastian out of the **Stay.** Have someone else enter the room, walk past him, then leave the room. Stand up, sit down, walk around the room, bend over, sit on the floor, get up, go back to him and release him with **Good stay!** and lots of praise.

Never call Sebastian to **Come** to you when he is in a **stay.** That teaches him to end the **Stay** by **coming** to you rather than waiting for you to return and release him. If you call him out of the **stay,** you must praise him for **coming,** and he never receives the praise for a **Good stay!** This can cause confusion because if the praise is for breaking the **Stay** by **coming,** why bother to **stay?**

If you must call Sebastian to you, teach the command **Wait**. **Stay** then means don't move until I return to you, and **wait** means don't move until I tell you what to do! Then you can tell him to **Come,** or **Sit** or **Down** or whatever, after a **wait.**

Since Sebastian already knows **stay,** teaching **wait** is very easy. It basically means the same thing except that you are not necessarily going to return to him.

Anytime you want to teach a new word that has the same, or similar, meaning as one he already knows, always say the new word first, *immediately* followed by the old one. The reason the new word always precedes the old one is because at first Sebastian will not react until he hears the familiar sound. If the new word is always followed by the old one he begins to anticipate the old word and starts to respond to the sound of the new one. Use your hand signal or make up a new one for the new word.

At first the command would be said **Wait/Stay!** Every time you say **Wait** you immediately say **Stay.** Once you notice that Sebastian is responding immediately when you say **Wait,** then **wait** has become a new word you can use. Remember, use **wait** when you will not return to Sebastian to give him another command and **stay** when he must not move until you go back to him and release him.

If he is in a **stay** and breaks it just as you are about to end the **Stay,** don't praise him for a **Good stay** at that moment. A verbal reprimand and a rapid **Sit! Stay! Good stay!** is better than allowing Sebastian to break the **Stay** and receive praise for it!

One last comment about **Stay**—your voice and body are very important. You must give this command with confidence. You and Sebastian are a team. You must transmit the right signals with your voice, your face, your hands and your body language—he's counting on you to help him succeed!

BODY LANGUAGE

A dog's senses are very different than those of humans. He smells things you cannot smell, hears sounds in ranges you cannot hear and sees movement you cannot see. He depends on his senses to detect prey by the scent of a trail, the slightest little sound, the flicker of a blade of grass, etc. Because of his sensitivity to movement and keen understanding of body language, he is very aware of the slightest gestures you make.

Sebastian sees everything in his world from a dog's point of view and interprets your human body language as if it were dog body language. Dogs don't communicate with words, but they do communicate with very explicit body language. We expect them to understand our words and do as we say, but humans rarely take the time to learn the language of dogs.

Your dog talks a mile a minute to you with his body and in all likelihood you never "hear" him! All these many years the dog has had the responsibility of learning our language—it's about time we humans learned about dog language.

SUBMISSION

Owners should recognize the body language of submission. Wiggling, piddling little worms of dogs are often created by owners not recognizing submissive postures and continuing to punish long after the dog has "apologized" the only way he knows how.

A submissive dog holds his head and front end down, his ears flat against his head, his gaze away from you and his tail tucked between his legs. He appears to crawl on his belly and his rear end moves from side to side. If that doesn't work, he may lie down on his side and lift a rear leg to expose his abdomen. If you still haven't recognized his submission, he may roll over on his back. And if that's still not enough for you, he may be on his back and dribbling a few drops of urine—the ultimate submission. He is trying to let you know that even though he does not understand what has offended you, he's sorry you're offended and submits to and recognizes your leadership.

Think about your house-training days. You found a puddle and yelled "You naughty dog!" The dog slinked down. (WHAT'S WRONG?) "Don't you ever learn?" The dog went onto his side and cocked a rear leg. (WHY ARE YOU ANGRY WITH ME?) "What a bad, bad dog!" The dog rolled over on his back. (I DON'T UNDERSTAND ANY OF THIS!) "You are the worst dog I ever saw!" The dog was on his back and dribbled a few drops of urine. (I STILL DON'T UNDERSTAND AND NOW I'M REALLY SCARED!) "Oh, you filthy beast—get out of here!"

When you miss the signs of submission from the pup, he becomes very confused. He submitted to you in every conceivable way known to him and nothing worked to appease you. He doesn't understand all of your words but he can tell from your facial expression, tone of voice and body posture that you are angry about something. Without the comprehension of spoken language, your words are just noise. You have taught him that the stimulant of a puddle in the room, combined with your arrival, means you are going to be angry and take it out on him, so he squirms up to you dribbling urine as he comes—instantly going into his submissive routine hoping you accept his "apologies for being alive"!

Another example of humans not recognizing submission is when someone says their dog chews up the house to get even with them for leaving him alone. They are sure he knows it's wrong because when he's

been chewing, "he looks guilty!" when they enter the house.

Dogs are not vengeful animals. Your dog does not say to himself, "The family has gone off again and left me alone! Who do they think they are? DARN! What can I do that will really make them mad? AH HA! I know! I'll chew up the couch!" A dog doesn't have thought processes like that—people do! People hold grudges and assume that dogs do as well.

When you leave your dog alone in the house, he may need to chew to burn off some energy or anxiety. He had access to the couch, it had the scent of the family on it, he got on it, scratched around to nest into it, loosened up the fabric and started to chew because no one ever *taught* him how to make proper choices about what he can and cannot chew.

The first time this happened he was probably punished by being dragged to the couch, having his face pushed into the mess and being spanked or yelled at. The next time he hears you coming home, he checks the territory to be sure all is well and finds couch stuffing on the floor. Remember, 1.6 seconds after he has done something it is already too late for punishment—the punishment is associated with what he is doing at that precise moment. He may have chewed the couch hours ago, and now he doesn't know where the stuffing came from. But he knows that loose couch stuffing means that you are angry and he is punished.

When he sees you enter the house, he crouches down with what you perceive as "guilt." Actually, it is more likely the fear and anxiety of being punished for something he doesn't understand and the knowledge that his "apologies" don't work with you!

Imagine yourself in a foreign country, where you don't speak the language. You know someone is very angry with you, because she is ranting and raving and shaking a finger in your face. You don't know what you did to offend her, and saying, "I'm sorry!" doesn't help because neither of you speak the same language. That evening you are at a party and who should walk in but that same person you had the encounter with earlier. You would very likely go to great lengths to avoid her all evening.

That is probably how your puppy feels when he "apologizes" but you just continue to reprimand. Dogs submit with body language—not with words. Humans would benefit greatly by learning to accept submission as quickly as dogs accept it from each other. When you make a mistake with your dog he quickly "forgives" you—do the same for him! Accept his "apologies," then *teach* him the rules so he can get it right the next time.

DOMINANCE

It is very rare for dogs to have a blood and guts battle for dominance—it is usually more bluff and noise than real go-for-the-kill fighting. No one has ever seen one dog put a choke chain around the neck of another and hang him by it to show him who was boss. Nor do dogs use rubber hoses, shock collars, pinch collars or any other torture devices invented by man to control dogs. Dogs display dominance and submission by their body language. You can use body language, facial expression, eye contact and tone of voice to establish dominance over your dog without scaring or beating him into submission.

Dogs must always rank beneath all humans. It doesn't matter who your dog perceives as the alpha as long as he perceives himself as the omega! There are several things you can do, using body language, to demonstrate to Sebastian that he ranks at the bottom of your family.

Sebastian should never be allowed to sleep on the bed with his humans. It may give him the feeling of equality or, worse yet, superiority, when he stands over a prone, sleeping human who doesn't challenge his dominant position. He should sleep on the floor next to your bed, in his crate or his dog bed, so that if he awakens and stands up, the humans are always positioned above him, strengthening their dominant status over the dog.

Never allow Sebastian to **walk** in front of you. He must always be by your side or behind you. When walking through doors, he must not be allowed to pass through first but must **wait** until after you have passed.

Always make him do something for you before giving him anything. If you want to pet him, make him **sit** first and pet him only briefly. Too much petting can overstimulate some dogs and cause biting. To receive a treat or a meal Sebastian should first **sit** and **stay** or **wait.** This concept of teaching a dog to say "PLEASE" by looking to you for leadership is the number one most important lesson he must learn. This alone can prevent or cure many of the problems people complain about most.

Play time should be games like retrieve where the dog must **drop** the ball, **sit** and **wait** before you throw it for him. Children should never play games with the dog on the floor. After all, you cannot teach a dog to play games like Parcheesi™ and Monopoly.™ Dog games are "playfighting," "playbarking," "playbiting," etc. Being on the floor together puts the dog and children on an equal level and children do not understand the dominant body language the dog may display toward them.

Have lots of teaching sessions with Sebastian and always include a few **stays** in the submissive **down** position. Placing Sebastian in a long **Down** and **Stay** while you are reading a book, watching television, etc., teaches him to be quiet and calm when you are relaxing. Because the **down** is a submissive posture, staying **down** for a long while next to you also demonstrates your dominance in a subtle but effective manner.

Be sure Sebastian is not allowed to self-feed, but is rather on a schedule of two feedings a day for life. It is a subtle reminder, twice a day, that you are the leader! With scheduled feedings, you can enjoy those wonderfully easy teaching times with the food bowl— such as **sit, wait, stay,** etc. He is dependent on you. You're in a power position that demonstrates reliable and fair leadership. When done *properly* you will notice that he has more respect for you and what you say because you are demonstrating your leadership in ways that he can clearly understand.

PLAY BOW

The play bow is your dog's way of inviting play. When Sebastian wants to play with you, his face may appear to be smiling. Don't confuse a smile with a snarl. When you or your dog snarl, the corners of the mouth are drawn forward, the upper lip wrinkles and the teeth show. A smile, on the other hand, causes the corners of the mouth to stretch back, with no wrinkles on the upper lip and the teeth showing. Notice that the teeth are displayed in both a snarl and a smile!

AMF

When Sebastian is in a play bow his front elbows are flat on the floor, his head is down almost touching the floor, his butt is high in the air and his tail is wagging like mad, maybe even wagging in circles. He may play bark and bounce around in this position and sometimes paw at you to get you to play with him.

To see how easy it is to communicate with your dog, try imitating this position. Be sure you protect your face and ears. Dogs sometimes play games by using their mouth and when you invite the play, he may try to chew on your hair! Get down on all fours, put your elbows flat on the floor, your head down between your elbows and your butt up in the air, and waggle your rear end a bit. Most dogs find it very difficult to resist this invitation to play.

THREATENING OR AGGRESSIVE STANCE

A dog displaying aggression is usually defending territory. He makes himself look large by standing squarely on all fours, possibly even up on his toes. He establishes and holds direct eye contact with his "opponent." The hair along the scruff of his neck and down his back stands up. His head is held high with the ears standing erect, or for flop-eared dogs, the ears come forward. His tail is held high and, if it moves, sways very stiffly. If the animal is moving, he walks slowly and stiffly. His lips may be in a snarl with teeth showing, and he may have a low, throaty growl.

If you come upon a dog behaving in this manner, do *not* maintain eye contact with the animal. Holding the eye contact is accepting the challenge from the dog and daring him to do something about it. Break the eye contact but keep the dog in your peripheral vision. While watching him peripherally,

keep your hands in sight and very *slowly* move away from the dog. Don't make any quick, jerky movements, just sidle away until the dog starts to relax his body a bit, then walk, don't run, away from him.

An aggressive dog does not necessarily want to bite. He gives lots of warning, such as his aggressive stance and growling. If you continue to approach, he will probably growl and snap at you to make you back off.

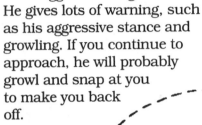

FEAR

A dog who threatens out of fear is even more dangerous than an aggressive dog. The aggressive dog gives lots of warning before actually biting. He growls, growls and snaps, and then maybe bites. But the fearful dog bites with no indication other than his body position.

His head is slightly lowered, his ears are back and flat against his head and he does not establish direct eye contact. His tail is either down, possibly swishing from side to side, or it's tucked between his legs. His body is crouched like a cat ready to lunge. You must not approach this dog too closely. Actually approaching may cause a sudden bite. The best thing to do is back away and let the dog approach you if he wants to.

A fearful dog is very unpredictable from day to day. It should not be brought into a household with children— it is just too risky.

Life Experiences

SOCIALIZING

Proper socialization is one of the most important tasks an owner has when bringing home a new puppy. At the age of seven weeks to four months, the puppy is in his socialization stage. During this time everything that happens to him has a lifelong effect. If he is well-socialized with lots of people and other animals, exposed to new environments and lots of stimuli, he will grow up to be confident and secure.

One sure way to accomplish proper and positive experiences during the socialization period is by attending a KPT class. There Sebastian is reintroduced to other puppies so he can continue his education as a dog. But he is also surrounded by and handled by lots of new people, in a new environment with new smells, sights and sounds. The more experiences a young puppy has during the socialization stage, the more "sophisticated" a dog he will grow up to be!

The worst case I ever saw of a non-socialized animal was a small dog owned by an older woman. She *never* took the puppy outside of her home or had visitors until the dog was over two years old. When her niece came to visit, the poor dog was terrified by this new person and every time she tried to get near him, he would growl and snap and keep backing up. At one point the niece had cornered the dog in an attempt to get hold of him and he bit her rather badly. I was shocked when I learned he was paper trained and never taken outdoors. She cannot even take him to the vet, because as soon as she opens her door the dog panics, digs in his heels and does not budge.

If she had brought her dog to KPT as a young pup, he would have had all sorts of experiences to build up his confidence. The socializing would have eliminated the fearful, shy, biting behaviors and getting to and from class would have prevented the fear of leaving the home.

During Sebastian's socialization stage, KPT can make a great difference in the kind of dog he'll grow up to be. At this age you are dealing with a little "airhead." His brain is like a sponge ready to soak up information. Since there is very little stored on the brain at this age, the data he is fed does not compete for storage space. What he learns during this period has the greatest impact on his life. He is learning all the time and learns more quickly than he ever will again.

PHYSICAL EXAMS AND HANDLING

Teach Sebastian to enjoy life while he is young and small. Sebastian must learn about such things as veterinarians, veterinary exams, grooming, children and being handled by strangers of all shapes, ages and sizes. You don't want your puppy to grow up aggressive, fearful, shy or "bitey," so make these life experiences fun and rewarding.

You don't have to be a veterinarian to do a veterinary exam. You don't even have to know what you are looking for—all you have to do is do it! Of course a little knowledge about the dog can be useful while doing this exercise. It's easier to know when Sebastian requires medical attention if you are familiar with how he normally looks and feels.

Sebastian should tolerate a physical exam by anyone. With Sebastian on his side, start with the ears. Since the veterinarian probably will use an otoscope, you can poke your fingertip (just the tip) into the ear to simulate the feeling of something going into the ear. Look into his ear, say **Ear! Good ear!** and feed him a treat. Check the other ear and repeat the same process. His ears should not be bright pink or flaming red, and there should be no heavy discharge or foul odor. If any of these conditions exist, he should see a veterinarian right away.

Next check his eyes. You can first look at the iris, the colored part of the eye, which is all that usually shows. It should be bright and clear without any cloudiness or opacities. Now using your thumb pull up on the upper lid to check the white of the eye, then down on the lower lid to check the conjunctiva. Say **Eye! Good eye!** as you feed him a treat. The white should be white, not all red and bloodshot, and the conjunctiva should be a light pink, not bright red or inflamed. One other thing you should notice—dogs have eyelashes only on the upper lid and the lashes should curl outward. If the upper lid curls inward and the lashes are scratching on the cornea when he blinks (a very painful condition) the dog must see a veterinarian immediately.

Next gently lift the upper lip so you can see Sebastian's teeth and gums. Say **Teeth! Good teeth!** as you do it. Then gently pry open his mouth so you can look in and down his throat and say **Mouth! Good mouth!** and reward him. Sebastian's teeth should not have cavities. It is sugar that causes cavities and he should never have sugar. But the teeth will eventually be stained by plaque and tartar that can lead to gum disease. At some point his teeth are going to need care. Either the veterinarian will have to do it under general anesthesia, or you can practice good dental care at home.

To accomplish this, accustom Sebastian to having his teeth touched by rubbing them with your finger and rewarding him when he lets you do it. Then wrap a piece of gauze around your finger to add the sensation of something rough on his teeth and rub that on his teeth. Next, wrap a rough washcloth around your finger and rub that over his teeth. At this point you can progress to the use of a soft, doggy toothbrush and some doggy toothpaste. Never use human toothpaste on a dog. The detergent in it is very harsh on their enamel and they do not rinse and spit, which means they swallow the toothpaste. This can cause an upset stomach and much displeasure about brushing the teeth. You can use a mixture of baking soda, salt, hydrogen peroxide and water mixed into a paste, or doggy toothpaste from the veterinarian or pet supply store.

Regular brushing daily or even three times a week will save you the expense of dental care by the veterinarian. But more importantly, it will save Sebastian the stress of general anesthesia and he will have shiny, white, healthy teeth that will make you, your veterinarian and Sebastian very proud!

Now gently rub your hands all over Sebastian's body as you tell him **Good dog! Good dog!. . . . .** You want to look for parasites and feel for lumps, bumps, bruises or cuts. Take each paw into your hand as you say **Paw! Good paw!** Squeeze gently on and between each toe. If you have a pair of pet nail clippers, just place them on the nail. Don't squeeze the clippers, just place them there and praise Sebastian as you feed him a treat and say **Nail! Good Nail!** This prepares him for having his nails clipped. Even if this is something you don't intend to do yourself, you should accustom Sebastian to the feel of clippers on his nails so when the groomer or veterinarian clips his nails, he doesn't bite or pull away.

All dogs need to have their nails clipped at one time or another. It is not done for aesthetics or because the nails clicking on the floor are making you crazy, but for Sebastian's well-being. As a dog's nails grow they curve down. The longer they become, the more uncomfortable it is for the dog to stand on them. This causes him to splay out his toes in an effort to relieve the discomfort. Splaying out the toes puts a great deal of stress and strain on the bones and joints and can actually lead to

early arthritic conditions.

Next, pull his tail up and say **Tail! Good tail!** The only way to take a dog's temperature is rectally—they simply will not cooperate and hold an oral thermometer under their tongue for a full five minutes! Normal rectal temperature is 101°F-102.5°F. Even if you don't take Sebastian's temperature he should tolerate his tail being pulled up without biting or being scared.

If Sebastian does act squirmy or "bitey" when you touch him or try to lift his tail, for example, back up! Instead of lifting the tail all the way, just touch it very gently, say **Tail! Good tail!** and feed him a treat. Do that several times until he tolerates it well. Then gently hold the tail between your fingers. Don't lift it yet. Say **Tail! Good tail!** and feed him a treat. When he doesn't balk at this, try gently lifting his tail a little, repeating the same process, until you can finally lift his tail all the way up and over his back.

This is done for any part of the body that causes fear or biting when touched. Make a game of it so Sebastian enjoys being gently touched anywhere on his body. Slowly progress to lifting, pulling, prying or whatever the case may be.

Notice that whatever part of the body you touch you tell Sebastian the name of the body part. If you ever have to put drops in his ears, for example, you can say **Ear!**, lift the earflap, put the drops in, say **Good ear!** and give him a treat. By teaching him the names of his body parts you can easily work on them by using the names as commands. That gives him some warning as to where you are going to touch him. He won't be frightened by a hand suddenly reaching out to lift his earflap!

Sebastian must learn to tolerate all kinds of handling by humans. Children can be very rough with a dog. They pinch skin, pull tails, pull ears, grab chunks of skin in their hands and twist, etc. If

Sebastian has not been taught to tolerate such behaviors he may lash out and bite the child in self defense.

On the other hand, if he is taught that tolerating discomforts at the hands of humans is fun and rewarding, rather than biting he looks for praise or reward. If a child is playing with Sebastian you don't have to be worried that the child might be bitten by him.

Another benefit is that when he is in pain and requires veterinary care, some minor treatments can be done without resorting to anesthesia or tranquilizers. How do you teach Sebastian to "enjoy" low level discomfort? It is very easy!

Make a game of it! Sit on the floor with him in your lap and one hand full of little treats. Gently pull his ear and feed him a treat. Now gently pinch the ear and feed him a treat. Now pull and pinch and feed him a treat. Keep on adding different levels of discomfort as you go.

When you reach a point where he responds to the discomfort and tries to bite or pull away, gently "growl" at him, repeat the last bit of handling he tolerated, reward him and let him go. Next time you play the game, start at the level that was last tolerated and slowly progress from there.

Do this all over Sebastian's body. Pinch his skin, twist it, pull the ears, pull the lips, pull the tail—do anything you think a child might do to your dog. Never let him go when he tries to bite. Instead, "growl" a reprimand and have him tolerate one more gentle pinch so you can reward him. Then the last image on his brain is you pinched him, he didn't lash out and you gave him a reward!

Now that Sebastian tolerates you doing these things to him, it is important that he tolerate it from other family members, friends and children, not only in his home environment but in other locations as well. After all, most veterinarians don't make house calls! Have as many different people as possible do the veterinary exam. If you don't have children, borrow some from a friend!

Your veterinarian will respect you and Sebastian if she can perform a simple exam or procedure without using a muzzle, tranquilizer, muscleman or anesthetic. No one wants to live with a dog who bites strangers or children just because he was touched. If all of this seems like too much trouble, remember a dog who bites is a dog who will die!

GROOMING

All dogs need some kind of grooming, but some dogs need extensive grooming done with blow dryers, clippers, scissors, etc. All dogs should learn to tolerate bathing, rubbing with a towel, brushing, combing, clipping nails, washing the face and wiping the paws. If Sebastian needs professional grooming, then he should also be introduced to the sound and feel of blow dryers, clippers and scissors.

Have all of the tools you will need—brush, comb, towel, nail clippers, washcloth and, if necessary, a blow dryer, clippers and scissors. You don't have to know how to use them on Sebastian or know anything about grooming. You just want to familiarize him with these items so he considers them fun rather then fearful.

It is very easy to accustom a dog to all of this—you just play the **grooming** game. Have some treats to reward him so he can make a pleasant association with being groomed. He can then think of it as a fun and rewarding game rather than an ungodly chore!

Now get on the floor with Sebastian. With the towel in one hand and the treats in the other, let him sniff at the towel, say **Towel! Good towel!** and reward him. Gently touch him with the towel as you repeat the words and feed the treat. Next gently and quickly wipe his face as

you say **Towel! Good towel!** and reward him. Slowly build up his tolerance to the towel until you can use it all over his body in a fashion that simulates drying a wet dog.

The next time you play the game, pretend to dry him off, then introduce the brush to him. Let Sebastian sniff at it as you say **Brush! Good brush!** and reward him. Touch him gently with the *back* side of the brush, not with the bristles—**Brush! Good brush!** and reward him. Gently rub the *back* side of the brush along his body and keep on repeating the words and rewarding him. Now turn it over and *very gently* make one swipe with it as you say **Brush! Good brush!** and feed him. Start out very gently, slowly building up the pressure you use until he tolerates being brushed.

Dogs who need professional grooming require further education. Even if you are not planning to do this kind of grooming yourself, it is very wise to introduce Sebastian to the tools of the trade before he goes to the grooming parlor. He will recognize the tools and the noise they make, and understand this is just the grooming game that you have played at home, so grooming won't be a fearful, traumatic experience.

Place a hair dryer on the floor and encourage Sebastian to come over to investigate it. If he just approaches the dryer reward him as you say **Dryer! Good dryer!** Let him move at his own pace to approach and investigate this new item. When he shows no fear, pick it up and hold it. Be sure you happily say **Dryer! Good dryer!** and reward him each time he makes even the slightest bit of progress.

Now plug it in, turn it on low, and direct the dryer away from Sebastian; happily talk to him and praise him for allowing the dryer to blow. Gradually change the direction of the dryer until it is actually blowing on him. Move very slowly as you progress each step.

To teach Sebastian about the noisy clippers use the same procedure you did with the dryer. When he is comfortable with the noise of the clippers, accustom him to being touched by them. With the blade removed, turn on the clippers and quickly and gently touch them to him. Say **Clippers! Good clippers!** and reward him. When he tolerates a gentle touch, you can try moving the clippers along his body, happily saying **Clippers! Good clippers!** and other words of encouragement as you reward him.

Next work with the scissors. They don't make electrical noises, but they do click, click along. Pick up the scissors and let Sebastian sniff at them. Say **Scissors! Good scissors!** and reward him just for sniffing. Then gently touch them to his coat. Don't do anything but touch him as you say the words and reward him. Now open and close them and let him watch, listen and sniff.

This may seem like more work than you want to do with your dog but I promise you it is worth it. I owned a dog many years before I knew about teaching life experiences. He was only 45 pounds but he was a pistol. It took five adult people to clip his nails—four of them to hold him down and one to clip. It was a struggle to put medication in his chronically infected ears and anyone who tried to pick him up risked a serious bite.

Now I own a 60-pound dog to whom I can do anything. I clip his nails by myself, administer medication without a struggle, pick him up and place him anywhere in any position. He thinks life is a real kick because everything has been presented to him as a game he can win and it was fun for both of us! All he has to do is relax, enjoy and trust and he is rewarded either with food, a smile, a hug, a kiss or the best reward of all for him, being allowed to jump up and give me a hug!

Learning about life should always be fun for both you and Sebastian. Present grooming in a happy, playful, positive manner and you won't have to struggle with a full-grown dog to do simple things like clip nails, clean ears, wipe muddy paws, administer medications and visit the veterinarian. If you put the time in now and subject Sebastian to the type of handling he must tolerate throughout his life, he'll always be easy to handle, groom, medicate and love!

THE FRIENDLY EATER

It may be cute to see a puppy "growl" at feeding time, but adult dogs with their powerful teeth are dangerous, not cute. If Sebastian is never taught to tolerate hands reaching for his bowl or to being petted, annoyed or talked to while eating, he may become very possessive and nasty about his feeding dish. That is dangerous, especially if children are in the home. Someone may "bother the dog while he is eating" and be bitten.

Teaching Sebastian to be a friendly eater who enjoys being touched and tolerates hands reaching for his bowl at feeding time is a simple process and well worth the effort. The mistake most people make is immediately attempting to take the bowl away from the dog. That is the goal but it is not the first step.

First, make him comfortable with people nearby as he eats. Accomplish this by sitting on the floor with your legs crossed. Place the food bowl in your lap and let Sebastian eat his entire meal from your lap while you pet and talk to him.

Next time place only a portion of his food in the bowl, sit on the floor with the bowl in your lap and let him eat from your lap. Just before he finishes, reach into the bowl with another handful of food. Keep feeding by handfuls until he completes the meal. Do this several times until he's comfortable being petted and seeing your hand reach into the bowl to deliver more food.

Now Sebastian is comfortable with your hand reaching for the bowl because your hand gives rather than takes away. Next, feed him just a handful of food in the bowl. When he's finished, raise the bowl and right in front of him place another handful of food into it. Put it back in your lap and let him eat. When he finishes that handful, again lift the bowl up and place more food into it. Keep repeating this until he finishes his meal. Pet him and talk to him while he is eating.

When Sebastian is comfortable with all of this, place his bowl on the floor with a handful of food in it. While he is eating, stroke and pet him. If he tolerates this very well, you may feed him a treat. When he finishes the handful of food, take his bowl away, place more food in it, put the bowl down and let him continue his meal.

Next, take the bowl away from him while there is still food in it. If he behaves nicely, feed him a tidbit or place a special treat into the bowl. If not, you have progressed too quickly. Back up to the last step he tolerated, work a little longer on that and then try to progress in smaller, slower steps. Remember to stroke him while he is eating.

It is also a good idea to teach Sebastian to **sit** and **wait** until he is released before he starts to eat. If necessary, use some food from his bowl to lure him into a **sit.** Tell him to **Wait** as you place the bowl down. If he dives right in, growl at him and take the bowl away. Try again. If he still does not **wait** until released, take the bowl away and put it out of reach. Try the procedure again in about 15 minutes.

Don't have him do a long **Wait** at first, just a second or two. You're teaching him not to lunge at food. You can start to extend the **Wait** when he gets the idea not to eat until told to. Be random about the length of time. If it's always short, he'll anticipate the release. Too long a **Wait** may become stressful. Being random helps Sebastian pay close attention to you as he **waits** for permission to eat!

When he does a **Wait** every time and tolerates hands reaching for him and his bowl, have other family members and friends join in. If children are in the house get them involved. Anyone, at any time, should be able to pet and stroke Sebastian, stand very close by while he eats, reach down to take the bowl away from him or place more food into the bowl without being threatened by a growly, biting dog.

Problem Solving

DOING WHAT COMES NATURALLY!

The dog is a urinating, defecating, biting, barking, chewing, digging, jumping machine. These are natural doggy behaviors. That cute, furry, wiggly little family member isn't aware that such acts displease you. If no one educates Sebastian, he does what comes naturally—he behaves like a dog. Then the owner complains because he perceives the dog as nothing but trouble.

Rather than take the time to teach him, he is banished to the yard or "gotten rid of" because the owner thinks he was a destructive, "untrainable" little beast! In this sense, teaching really can save Sebastian's life. It is up to the family to humanely teach Sebastian how to behave with his humans rather than punish him for behaving like a dog.

Actually his behaviors, in and of themselves, are not problems. The problem is really the where, when, what, and why of the behavior. Remember, you cannot solve the problem until you *properly* define the problem:

1. Urinating/defecating: All living creatures must do these bodily functions. You're not upset because your dog urinates and defecates. You don't want to stop him from performing these necessities. The problem is not that he must eliminate. It's where and when he eliminates. It is your responsibility to teach him both where his toilet area is and to hold it until he can get there. Then he can live in the home and be an acceptable family member.

2. Chewing: Dogs like to chew—puppies need to chew. Chewing is fun! It feels good and helps relieve stress and anxiety. Chewing is not the problem—it's what the dog selects to chew. Provide Sebastian with a

chew toy such as a Nylabone®. When properly taught what he can and cannot chew he can still behave like a dog without being a problem chewer.

Babies and puppies must be taught how to survive in the world. The parents' responsibility is to raise and teach their child what she must know. A human baby is born with a brain programmed to receive and interpret human data. No one would expect a baby to learn, all by herself, the information necessary to survive in society.

Then why expect a baby dog to know how to please his human family? The poor puppy has a brain ready to receive doggy information but must learn to cope and exist in a world of humans. It is up to the humans to teach the dog all he must know in order to be a family pet, not a pest! The people must understand what a dog is—not the other way around.

It is a credit to the dog that all these eons he has been able to adapt to our ways. He has done an exceptionally good job of it considering most humans still don't understand dogs. All doggy behaviors humans consider problems are no problem to the dog—they are what comes naturally!

HOME IS WHERE THE DOG IS!

Why bring Sebastian inside the home? Because that's where he belongs. Dogs are very social animals and they need to be part of a family group. It is up to the family to teach the dog proper behavior. If he is not *taught* rules he will make up his own and just do the best he can. There is only one thing he knows how to be—a dog!

Dogs are pack animals. A pack is not a chaotic group of dogs, but rather a ranked hierarchy with very strict rules. Dogs respect leadership. Every pack *must* have a leader—this is not an option to the dog. If no human capably takes on the role, the dog is *obligated* to become leader and rule the house. Misbehavior does not mean the dog is stupid or spiteful. It means the dog doesn't understand the rules, isn't sure of his position in the family or has the misconception that he's the leader. When the dog consistently "misbehaves," most people decide he must live outside.

The person who banishes the dog to the yard and won't solve simple indoor problems certainly will not take the time to solve outdoor problems. So the next step is tie up the dog all day and night or "get rid of the dog." Such a person would have been better off getting a potted plant that would happily sit outside all day— this person had no business getting a dog!

People who buy a house with a yard, then get a dog and expect the dog to be happy all alone in the yard, are unrealistic. The "outside dog" has many lonely, long, boring hours that just drag by. To release the stress, tension and frustration, the dog will do whatever helps him to feel better! Living a life of solitary confinement in the back yard is actually a form of cruelty and abuse—isolation is a very severe form of punishment.

A family dog should not be part of your landscaping. He should be part of the family. When Sebastian lives in the house he is always close by. It is easier to catch him in the act of making a mistake so you can stop the behavior and instruct him as to what he should have done. A dog who lives in the home and has been taught the rules is an acceptable family member.

Because you spend more time with him, you derive the benefits of living with a dog, such as: he learns more words and learns them more quickly; your blood pressure is lowered by his presence; you have companionship; he alerts you to danger and gives you non-judgmental love; and you bond with each other and learn about, and from, each other, just to name a few.

THE PROCESS OF ELIMINATION

More dogs are beaten and/or euthanized for soiling in the house than for any other behavior problem, including biting. People make excuses for biting, such as he doesn't like men with beards, he's nervous around tall people, he doesn't like his tail touched, etc. These same people will beat a dog, "rub his nose in it," exile him to the back yard or "get rid of the dog" just because he does the most natural of acts—elimination.

People make teaching the *process of elimination* more difficult than it has to be. When most people take the dog outside they pay a great deal of attention to him *until* he finally "goes to the bathroom." They talk to him and play with him—COME ON, PHYDEAU! HURRY UP NOW! LET'S GO!, etc. When the dog eliminates, they say GOOD DOG! and go back into the house.

From the dog's point of view, this might seem like punishment for having "gone to the bathroom." Until he eliminated, all of the attention was focused on him—he was the center of the universe. Then he squatted, some words were spoken, he was brought into the house and then ignored. The dog learns that as soon as he eliminates he loses the attention. So, he holds it longer and longer, until the owner has been outside for more than an hour "playing" with the dog. When she finally quits "playing" and brings him in the house, he immediately puddles on the rug because he's been holding it all that time while playing!

Reverse your behavior. Pay no attention to Sebastian until he "goes to the bathroom." Then reward him with a treat and maybe a game of retrieve.

The Process of Elimination

The *process of elimination* is not a problem of urination and defecation. All dogs must urinate and defecate. These are normal body functions for *all* living beings. Your dog would die if he could never urinate and defecate. Teaching the *process* of elimination actually entails the following:

1. LOCATION—Don't go inside the house; go outside.
2. COMMUNICATION—"Let me *know* when you have to go and I will let you outside." It's of no value if the dog stands by the back door but doesn't let you know he's there!

Dogs are clean animals. Newborn puppies don't have an elimination reflex because, if 10 puppies were all urinating and defecating in the den whenever they got the urge, there would be no way for Mother to keep a clean "house." The Mother dog actually teaches the puppies to eliminate when she licks at the anal and genital area to clean them after they nurse. She ingests their bodily wastes in order to keep the "house" clean.

At about three weeks of age the pups' eyes and ears are functioning and they move about more. When they have the urge to eliminate, they instinctively crawl away from the den in order to do their necessities. The four times puppies usually have to eliminate are:

1. When they first wake up in the morning.
2. After they eat or drink.
3. During and/or after play or exercise.
4. When they wake up from a nap.

You can use this information when teaching the *process of elimination.* It is apparent that a normal, healthy dog will not eliminate where he sleeps. Sebastian has probably never soiled in his bed and continued to sleep there. Most owners give puppies too much freedom too quickly. Confinement is the name of the game when teaching the *process of elimination.*

CRATE! GOOD CRATE!

The easiest and quickest way to teach the *process of elimination* is by *properly* confining Sebastian with a wire crate. Please don't think of a crate as a cage—that is your perception of the crate (unless it's used inhumanely to confine the puppy in the crate in a room by himself or when no one is home). Puppies usually walk right into the crate with little or no coaxing.

No responsible parent would let a baby crawl around the house unattended. The infant would be in a safe place, such as a crib or playpen. This should also be true for puppies and dogs. A crate is Sebastian's safe area and bed when his humans are home but too busy or unable to watch him.

There are many advantages to crate teaching Sebastian. Travelling in a crate is extremely safe and a little piece of familiarity for him in a strange place. When you drive, a safe place for your dog would be in a securely fastened crate—no dog is safe roaming free in a vehicle! Many hotels and motels that are not fond of pets will often make an exception if the pet is crated. They don't have to worry about puddles on the rug, chewing, or surprising the maid! Also, if Sebastian spends a night at the veterinary hospital, he'll most definitely be crated. If he's accustomed to a crate he'll relax and heal but if he's never experienced this before, he may panic and do serious harm to himself.

The crate should be a dog's safe haven—a good place for napping, resting, being alone when he has the need or recuperating from an illness. A crate is never used for punishment or anything negative. Never put a crated dog outdoors, in the garage, in the basement or in the house and then leave home. The crate would be too confining and could become an object of fear causing more problems than it solves. Children must *never* be allowed inside the puppy's crate. This is his "room" in the house. He deserves some privacy and quiet time when he needs it.

For teaching the *process of elimination* and confinement in the house, it is best to use a wire crate instead of a plastic or fiberglass one. Wire crates allow the dog a full 360 degrees of vision and have good air circulation. The crate should be bought large enough for the full grown dog. But the puppy must have only enough room to comfortably stand up, lie down, sit up, stretch and turn around in the crate. Section off this space using masonite, pegboard, corrugated fiberglass, etc., expanding the space as Sebastian grows.

When you bring the crate home, teach Sebastian to use it by playing **crate** games. Place the crate on the floor with the door open and sit down by it. Have some treats and place one right outside the entrance.

When he takes the treat say **Crate! Good crate!** You are teaching a "word" that later can be used as a command. Place another treat just inside the crate and again repeat **Crate! Good crate!** when he takes it. Keep moving the treat further and further into the crate until Sebastian refuses to go that far. At this point, place the treat at the last successful distance, let him take the treat, say **Crate! Good crate!** and let him go off to play.

About an hour or so later play the game again starting where you left off and continue doing this until Sebastian is going all the way into the crate. In a very short while he is walking in and out of his crate. When he's comfortable with this part of the teaching add the concept of the door.

Teach him that the door closes but it also opens. Lure Sebastian into the crate and close the door behind him. As soon as he turns around and sees it's closed, open it! Play this game a few times until he's comfortable with the door.

Now add the concept of time. Lure him into the crate, close the door behind him and leave it closed while you try to count to five. If he is quiet let him out. If he starts barking or whining give an instructive reprimand to make him be quiet. You can growl, rattle a shaker can, gently spray water, blow a whistle, stomp your feet, clap your hands—just make him stop the noise. When he's quiet, open the door. Don't make a big fuss over him right away—he may associate your attention with the door opening, and that's too much reward just for getting out. Move away from the crate before you greet him.

WHEN YOU CAN'T WATCH THE DOG...

When you're home and *not watching* Sebastian, he should be in his crate in the room with you. From your point of view, the whole house must be respected and, therefore, is off limits for toileting. But from the dog's point of view, the space where he sleeps is all that he must respect. The rest of your house is a toilet! When Sebastian is in the crate, he's in his "own room" and is therefore being set up to succeed rather than fail. Sebastian must be allowed in all the rooms of your home if he is to respect your entire house. By having him crated in the room with you, he's not able to eliminate just anywhere. He is also being taught that all rooms in the house are off limits for urination and defecation.

Remember, he has only enough room to comfortably stand up, lie down, sit up, stretch and turn around in the crate. When his bladder gets full and he feels the pressure signaling the urge to urinate, he'll start to cry, whine, bark, scratch or dig. This crying or whining sounds different than the sounds to be let out to play! You will eventually be able to distinguish the difference between these sounds, just as any parent can recognize different cries from a baby. Because the puppy is with you most of the time, it shouldn't take very long to know when to reprimand and when to let him out.

When he signals his needs, you must stop whatever you're doing, open the crate door, tell him **Outside!**—another "word" to add to his vocabulary of commands as long as it means the *same* door every time—then *go outside with him.* Just stand there, ignoring him, for about five minutes. If he doesn't eliminate during those five minutes, take him back in and put him in the crate. About 15 minutes later say **Outside!** and go out with him. If during this time he eliminates, go to him, praise him, feed him a treat, then stay outside another five minutes and play with him. Teach him that the sooner he eliminates, the sooner you play with him—no elimination, no play time!

CAUGHT IN THE ACT...

When you're home watching Sebastian it means your eyes are on him. You're not looking through a magazine, periodically glancing at the dog. You're focused directly on the dog! When he suddenly exhibits behavior indicating he has to eliminate (he's sniffing at the floor, his tail's rising, he's walking in circles and suddenly he squats) *don't get mad, get glad!* Keep your sense of humor—this is a perfect opportunity to teach your dog.

You must show him that urination and defecation are not bad—it's his choice of location that makes you angry. After thanking your lucky stars for this opportunity to teach the dog, scream a blood curdling *AHHHHHHHHHHHHHHHHHHHHHHHHHHHH!!!!!* to startle him so every muscle in his body will constrict. He'll stop what he's doing, leaving some urine in his bladder or feces in his bowels. Then say **Outside!** and dash Sebastian out the door that leads to his toilet area. Remember, always use the *same* door. You can attach his leash, walk him or nudge him—whatever works best—but don't carry him. The more he does by himself the sooner he learns his lessons. Try to eventually work him up to walking on his own, straight to the door.

Go outside with him. While he's squatting outside, you can softly say something like **Hurry up!** to teach him more new "words". **Hurry up!** can later be used to have Sebastian eliminate on command when you're in a hurry. As soon as he finishes his business outside, praise him—and feed him a tidbit! He'll probably think you've snapped your lid. Your neighbors will surely wonder what caused such a horrendous scream at your house. You have just enjoyed a perfect teaching interaction with your dog.

He may be a little confused at first—"What is going on? I must be living with a really crazy family! They scream when I squat in the house, then feed me treats for the same act out here." But that's precisely the message you want to send. It is not urinating or defecating that upsets you. It's Sebastian's choice of location. Make it worth his while to do these acts outside because he gets a treat and some play time, and he'll want to save up his toileting needs until he can get outside to do them!

THE LIGHTS ARE ON, BUT NO ONE IS HOME...

Don't leave Sebastian outside while you're gone. A puppy left outdoors all day is at great risk from sudden changes in the weather, dog nappers, children harassing him, escaping, gates inadvertently left open, etc. The outdoor habits of digging, barking and escaping—problems that stem from the boredom and frustration of isolation—are far more difficult to solve than the indoor problems of house soiling and chewing.

Leaving him outside actually makes teaching the *process of elimination* more difficult and time consuming. When he's outdoors, the muscle control, required to hold his toileting needs for any length of time, is not developed because he eliminates whenever and wherever he gets the urge. Plus he receives no rewards for all the "duties" performed in the yard.

Sebastian should be confined to the kitchen. (Bathrooms are too small and difficult to puppy proof.) Kitchens usually have linoleum or tile floors that clean easily, are roomy and easy to "puppy proof." Remove the mop and broom between the refrigerator and counter, the mat in front of the sink, the towels hanging from the refrigerator door, the trash can, all items on the edge of the counter, etc. Temporary barriers of "puppy gates" or peg board slipped into runners can be put up to block entry ways.

Sebastian should have access to his crate with the door wired open, a bowl of water and his chew toys.

When you arrive home, if you find some puddles and piles, they are only on the kitchen floor. There are no surprises squishing between your toes in the bedroom!

Immediately take him outside for five minutes. If he eliminates, praise him and play with him. If he doesn't, just bring him back in and place him in his crate. Even if he did toilet outside, put him where he cannot watch you cleaning the kitchen floor. If he watches you clean up his mess, he may try to "clean up" by eating it—a most disgusting habit called coprophagia! Clean up the kitchen with a 50-50 white vinegar and water solution, then use one of the stronger odor neutralizers from a pet supply store to really eliminate the odor. It is the smell of his own urine that keeps Sebastian "going" in the same place!

THE FOOD CONNECTION...

Notice that no food is left for Sebastian. When the puppy has access to food all day, teaching the *process of elimination* is extremely difficult. Every time he eats he has what's called a gastrocolic reflex—the act of swallowing food starts muscle contractions all through his digestive tract and finally out the bowel. Every time he eats a meal, he has a bowel movement—if he eats many small meals he has many bowel movements. Since you don't know when Sebastian last ate, you can't know when he needs to eliminate. You're not in control!

On scheduled feedings, your puppy is under your control. Because of the gastrocolic reflex, you can practically time his bowel movements by noting how soon after he eats he has a bowel movement. If you know that 20 minutes after he eats, he has to eliminate, then you can schedule his feedings so he defecates before you leave for work or go to bed.

A feeding schedule of two feedings a day for life can cut down on hyperactivity. When the dog eats, food is

AMF

in his stomach for about five hours. On one feeding, that leaves 19 straight hours every day with no food in the stomach. On two feedings, there is food in the stomach for 10 hours every day and the 14 hours without food are broken up into shorter time periods.

What your pet is fed also affects the *process of elimination.* Grocery store products usually are not as nutritious and have more filler than premium foods. Dogs eat more grocery store food, less of it is used by the body and, thus, more stool is produced. Premium foods appear to cost more but they last longer because Sebastian eats less to get his nutritional needs met. Because he eats less, the extra cost probably evens out in the long run. More of the food is assimilated by his body, producing smaller, firmer stool. Small, firm stool is like a gift from the heavens when teaching the *process of elimination!*

THE LATE, LATE SHOW...

At bedtime, Sebastian should sleep in the adults' bedroom, on the floor, in the crate—not in the children's room. Children are not dependable enough to get up in the middle of the night to take the puppy outside. Adults usually sleep with one eye and one ear open all night, ready to get up when needed.

At three o'clock in the morning, when the puppy cries to go potty, someone must get up, take him outside, praise him for going, come in and put him back in his crate. You don't have to do this forever. By 12 weeks of age puppies can usually sleep through the night.

With this method of teaching, puddles and piles on the carpet are really your fault. Any squishy surprises are not his fault. If he had urine in his bladder or feces in his bowels, why was he uncrated when no one was watching him? Sebastian should never be running around free without someone watching him unless he has been observed emptying both the bladder and the bowel. When both systems are empty then he can be free and unattended for at most one hour.

Teaching the *process of elimination* can be completed in a relatively short period of time. Usually within two to six weeks, Sebastian should have the rules down pat. The problem is that most puppies are not physically capable of holding their bladders for long periods of time until they're four to six months of age. So expect some puddles until he is physically capable of lasting an eight to ten hour day without any accidents! Remember, Sebastian is not trying to upset you—he's just doing the best he can under the circumstances.

Chewing

CHEWING

Dogs chew, that's nothing new. Chewing is normal healthy dog behavior. Even people like to chew gum! Yet it's a behavior that gets dogs into trouble. People don't appreciate chewed up furniture, clothes, carpets, floors, doors, cabinets, walls, shoes, bedspreads or any other item his teeth may munch on. The problem is not that Sebastian is chewing but rather *what* he is "chewsing." You wouldn't care if he chewed until he had no teeth left, if he chewed his own toys! Remember it's your responsibility to set up success rather than failure—if he chews your slipper, ask yourself why the slipper was left where he could get it!

Chewing is a typical doggy pastime. In the wild, when a mother dog starts to wean her pups, she spends more time standing up with her teats out of reach. She leaves the nest more often to hunt. Upon her return, the pups smell food on her breath and lick at her mouth until she regurgitates so they can lap it up. In this way they learn about eating solid foods. Next, she and other pack members leave chunks of food around the immediate vicinity of the den. These "gifts" are for the pups to practice playhunting and playkilling and finally to eat.

When you leave your possessions within Sebastian's reach, from the dog's point of view, it appears that you left him a "gift" to playhunt, playkill, and attempt to eat. The obvious solution for some chewing problems is *don't* leave items where the dog can get them. He shouldn't have access to precious possessions. This is most easily accomplished by placing personal items up high, putting them into closets and cupboards or by closing doors.

Chewing

The problem of chewing, like most problems, is being able to catch the dog in the act. Remember, 1.6 seconds after the event is already too late for punishment. Sebastian chews your things because he's attracted by the familiar scent of the family on them and you left him with access to them. He needs something to do to release anxiety, burn off energy or pass the time of day. He can't watch television, read a book or knit himself a sweater, so he chews. This is "recreational" chewing. When you return home it's too late to save the item or punish him. It's up to you to teach Sebastian to use his chew toys and leave your "toys" alone.

You must be sure that you choose only safe and sane toys. The most common toys are made of rawhide and are really *bad* and *unsafe.* Rawhide, like leather, is made of hide. The dog may generalize and believe it's o.k. to chew all hides. Shoes, chairs, purses, gloves, jackets and belts can be leather! Chewed rawhide becomes very soft and mushy. Dogs can chew off and swallow a large piece, causing choking or an intestinal blockage—life threatening situations. Each time the dog chews rawhide he changes the configuration or actually devours the entire object. Either way, it's difficult to develop a sense of ownership about an item that changes or completely disappears!

Vinyl toys can also be very dangerous for an avid chewer. Most of them have squeakers. That's usually the first thing the dog removes and swallows. Vinyl can be shredded, and dogs can swallow large chunks and suffer the same fate as with rawhide. Most vinyl toys are in the shape of objects dogs shouldn't chew—shoes, sneakers, newspapers, hot dogs, hamburgers, chops, etc. It's all very confusing and confusion always leads to trouble.

An old pair of shoes, a knotted sock, a dish towel, a stuffed toy, etc., may appear to be good toys. But

NEVER CAN HAVE ENOUGH

NYLAFUN!

AMF

consider the high level of human thought required to distinguish an old, beat-up shoe from a new one. To the dog a shoe is a shoe is a shoe!

Balls, frisbees, dumbbells, etc., are not chew toys. These are "interactional" toys. They're used to play games with Sebastian such as catch, retrieve, find, etc. Frisbees® manufactured by the Nylabone® folks are the safest and most durable flying disc available. These scented discs are designed for dogs and will outlast other discs without question. These aren't items he should be allowed to keep and chew. When you're finished playing, the "interactional" toy should be placed out of his reach!

There are currently a number of chew toys that I consider to be excellent and safe. None of these look or smell like anything you wouldn't want the dog to touch. Nylon bones are made of a very hard plastic. When

Chewing

Sebastian chews on them he gets small shavings that become roughage in the system. The resulting bristles on the toy act as a toothbrush, cleaning his teeth when he chews. Some dogs may not show an interest in these toys. If that's the case, rough up the nylon bone with sandpaper or a file and let it soak overnight in some leftover soup, sauce or stew. When you present the bone the next day he should be very interested. Among the nylon bones available at pet shops, the Nylabone® is the most reliable as it's the original. Other nylon toys simply do not compare.

The sterilized beef bone is a good toy that can be bought in a pet supply store. They can be difficult to find, so ask the store owner to supply them. Sterilized bones have no fat or meat on them to go rancid, attracting flies or other insects. They're extremely hard, last a long time, and are safe. One of the best features is that they are hollow. You can stuff a little piece of food into the center, then rub the smell all over the outside of the bone. Present the stuffed bone to Sebastian before you leave. With the bone in his mouth, you increase the likelihood he'll chew it rather than a forbidden item.

The two most active chewing periods are right after you leave the house and just before your anticipated return because these are the two most anxious periods of the day. When you leave he's suddenly all alone and he's not sure you'll be back. Although he cannot read a clock, Sebastian has a marvelous sense of timing and he anticipates your usual arrival with joy and excitement (or fear if you punish him when you return).

When you arrive home, have him find the bone. By focusing attention on his chew toy when you arrive and denying him a greeting until the bone is in his mouth, you are teaching Sebastian to look for the bone before your arrival. Since that is an active chewing time, you increase the probability that he'll "chewse" the bone.

Poke the food out in front of him to demonstrate your powerful leadership. After all, he spent the day trying to get it out and couldn't. Feed him the tidbit to demonstrate that you're not only powerful but fair! Giving him the treat keeps him challenged, not frustrated, by the toy!

How many toys the dog has is important. When you limit his toys to only two different kinds, the results are very quick. If you increase the number to three toys, you will still have good results but it will take a little longer. Four or more different toys is too many because the dog then generalizes that he owns everything in your house!

I remember a case where a client called because her dog was chewing up brand new carpeting. Her husband was threatening to shoot the little beetle! I visited her home and asked to see the dog's "chewies." The lady returned with a laundry basket brimming with toys—there must have been over 50 of them—all of these wonderful items and the dog inevitably "chewses" the carpeting! As soon as I saw the basket I knew what the problem was—too many different toys.

There was no way to teach her dog to remember these 50 things were his and that the 51st item he touched would be a mistake. That's just too much for him to remember! He couldn't distinguish between dog toys and people toys! I had the owner obtain three approved items and teach her dog what to chew and what not to chew. That was the end of the problem!

Most people believe when the puppy has a forbidden object in his mouth they must exchange that item for a "chewie." The problem with this procedure is the dog has already made an incorrect choice, has the forbidden object in his mouth and then is rewarded by the attention he receives and an acceptable toy to chew on. He is not taught what his chewies are and to make correct choices on his own. The rules of chewing are:

133

Chewing

1. Chewing is o.k.
2. The dog can chew his toys and must leave people "toys" alone.
3. The dog must know what his toys are and "chewse" only those objects.

Teach the rules of chewing by playing the **Chewing** game! The intent is to catch Sebastian in the *act of putting his mouth on* a forbidden object and instructively reprimand him to **Drop!** it. Then let him make another choice. If Sebastian is the kind of dog who grabs an object and quickly runs off, tie a soft cord to his collar. Attach the other end to your foot so he can't get very far! Be sure not to use the leash, because he will get too excited thinking that he is going for a **walk!**

Sitting on the floor is an invitation to play. So sit on the floor with the three acceptable chew toys you have chosen for Sabastian and three objects you don't want him to chew. For example, you have a shoe, a sock, a (non-toxic) plant and the three acceptable toys. Sebastian comes to you and starts to sniff the items. Sniffing must be allowed. You choose objects based on looks but he makes choices based on smells.

Let's say Sebastian chooses the shoe. Instructively reprimand him with AHHHHHHHHHHHHH! **Drop! Good drop!** Then mix up the items and let him choose again. This time he chooses the sterilized bone. Say **Toy! Good toy!** and trade the bone for a treat and continue playing the game. Or end the game by letting him go off and chew on the bone. That's a great reward for having made a correct choice.

Every time you play, the only constants are the three acceptable items. You can change the others, or not, as you choose. Play this game for about five minutes at a time. The more often you play, the sooner Sebastian learns to earn praise or reward by "chewsing" one of his three toys. This teaches him to make proper choices on his own without depending on his humans to exchange good chewies for bad ones. The game is a *set-up* to catch him in the act of a mistake, but it's fair because he can make a correct choice and be a winner.

In the beginning, it's advisable to invest in quite a few of these toys. Have them in every room of the house, even outdoors. That way, wherever Sebastian is, he has access to a proper chew item and doesn't have to remember where he left his toys. As he gets older he'll remember where his "chewies" are and when asked to get a **toy** will run right to it. Regardless of how much you may spend on toys, it certainly costs less than having to replace all of your furniture!

Playbiting

PLAYBITING

I am not going to discuss aggressive or fear-induced biting. These problems are serious and potentially dangerous. Trying to cure them by reading a book is asking for more trouble. If your dog is a fear or aggression biter you need professional one-on-one counseling. Be sure to ask what methods are used. Steer clear of anyone suggesting punishment, pain, shock or violence as a deterrent. These techniques usually make the situation worse—after all, violence begets violence!

Never, never, never play tug-o-war games with a family dog of any age who hasn't been taught bite control. On the surface, tug-o-war seems like an innocent solution to the dilemma of playing with a puppy without being bitten. In actuality, it's extremely dangerous.

Think about the dynamics of the game. The owner holds one end of a rag and waggles the other in the dog's face. He grabs it with his mouth then tugs. The first time, the puppy probably loses his end of the rag. Then the owner waggles it again. Now he takes it and holds on really tight with his teeth. He tugs, bites harder and harder and receives no reprimands for his tenacious grip. Since your hand is at the other end of the rag, the dog is being taught to bite very hard and not let go when human hands are involved. Such lessons should never be taught to a puppy who must learn to be a family dog.

If Sebastian is biting like crazy, relax. If not, make him "playbite." A puppy who isn't playbiting is potentially dangerous. When puppies are together they don't play Parcheesi™ or Monopoly™. They play biting games to learn "bite control." It's very important for the puppy to know where his mouth is, where it will land and how hard to press when he bites. That's why puppies who "playbite" are safe and normal! It's very important that puppies "playbite" with their baby teeth.

The reason Sebastian's baby teeth are needle sharp is so they will hurt quickly! Although these teeth are very sharp, they're quite powerless. No one gets serious wounds, gashes or torn flesh from puppy teeth. However, the adult teeth, though dull, are very powerful. It's much easier to teach Sebastian about "bite control" when he has the powerless puppy teeth. If he already has his adult teeth, you still must teach him to control his bite but you must be very, very careful! A dog's mouth is a powerful biting machine that must be respected and understood.

If a dog intends to bite, even speedy reflexes won't prevent the bite. When a dog gives a warning snap, his mouth retreats even before a person can react because he has no intention of biting. Dogs have to develop precision when biting. They can't accidentally bite a pack member but they must precisely bite their prey in order to kill it. Consider a pack of dogs out hunting—if they can't compensate for movement, their mouths won't land on the prey. They'd die of starvation. They learn this control and precision by playing biting games as young puppies.

When puppies bite each other too hard, the one bitten usually yelps, then won't play for a few moments. The yelp is a distraction that stops the biting. The punishment is the withdrawal from play. After a few moments the pups play again so the biter can learn to bite softly enough to keep the play going.

The problem is that puppies tolerate harder biting than humans want to.

The best "toy" for teaching bite control is the human

hand. It's sensitive enough to detect slight touches, and a quick response from you teaches the dog not to use his mouth on humans. Don't smack Sebastian in the face, flick his nose or pinch his ears—all of these actions may cause reflexive biting. Don't stop him from using his mouth on you at first. If you do that, you can't teach him about "bite control." Instead, react to the slightest feel of teeth on your hands with a high-pitched, squeeky "OWWW!" *before* you feel pressure, then just ignore him for 30 seconds or so. This "yelp" distracts him so he stops biting—the withdrawal from play is the punishment for biting too hard. Teach Sebastian not to exert any pressure on your flesh in order to keep the play session going.

When the pressure disappears, then teach him not to put his mouth on you. As soon as you feel his mouth—even the slightest, gentlest touch—put on a Sarah Bernhardt performance: "Ow! Oh! That really hurt! Oh my gosh! The pain is awful!" All the while hold your hand and have a pained look on your face.

Sometimes, "yelping" may cause a rambunctious puppy to become excited and playful rather than to back off. If you've yelped three times and, rather than waiting for an invitation to play, Sebastian immediately comes back for more, you may have to isolate him.

Bring the puppy to his room gently and calmly place him in his crate and leave him alone for about 15 minutes. Then release him from the crate. Don't make a big deal about the release. Just ignore him for a short while, then calmly greet him and let him be. Do not initiate play for at least one hour. This usually subdues most puppies.

There is *never* an acceptable excuse for a family dog to bite. Teach Sebastian "bite control" as a young puppy, reinforce his learning throughout his life and he should never bite on human flesh.

JUMPING

Why does Sebastian jump? One reason is when dogs greet each other they usually do a "head sniff" in order to get a whiff of each other's breath. Where is your head? All the way at the top of your body. How is Sebastian going to get a whiff of your breath? He has to jump up. Obviously, one way to avoid the jumping is for you to kneel down, getting your head lower, so he doesn't have to jump.

Actually, most dogs jump because people unknowingly and unintentionally teach them to. When the dog is sitting, standing, or lying down he is usually ignored. In order to get some attention, he may jump on you. When he does that, he's usually pushed away, kneed in the chest, his feet are stepped on or some other "punishment" is inflicted while he is told, "Sebastian, get off!"

People see this as teaching the dog not to jump. However, from the dog's point of view, he has just received the attention he was looking for. He was touched—dogs love to be touched or pushed, try it on your dog and watch him come back for more. He was talked to but the only word he probably understood was his name, Sebastian. The rest was just "blah, blah, blah!" If you see yourself in this example, don't despair; it just proves what a good teacher you are already, what a good learner Sebastian is and that positive reinforcement really works!

The positive reinforcement approach is to ignore the dog totally when he is jumping: don't look, touch or talk to him. When all four feet are on the floor, either in a **sit, stand,** or **down,** the dog receives a quick pat, a word of praise and maybe even a favorite treat.

Jumping

Sometimes just ignoring is not enough. You may have to fold your arms across your chest and just totally walk away. When you walk away, try backing up quickly, causing him to drop his front paws onto the floor, then you can pet him and talk to him.

Everyone in the family must totally ignore the jumping. Consistency is an absolute must when teaching rules to Sebastian. If even one family member reacts only sometimes to the jumping, he is being intermittently reinforced, and knowing that it works at least some of the time, he will continue to jump.

Once Sebastian stops jumping on the family, invite some friends over to help teach him that jumping doesn't work on anyone. Inform your friends they should not wear good clothes because you are going to allow Sebastian to jump on them and they are to totally ignore him when that happens. When he has four feet on the floor, they should pet him, talk to him, even feed him a tidbit.

Remember to pet him, talk to him and look at him when he is not jumping. If you pay attention to Sebastian only when he misbehaves you are teaching him that misbehavior is a good way to get your attention. It is better to teach him to get your attention with behavior that pleases you by always praising Sebastian when he does something right. He must learn *your* definition of good behavior before he can learn not to "mess up."

BARKING

Dogs bark! It's natural for Sebastian to bark—you don't expect him to moo like a cow, do you? If a person talks too much, no one becomes violent or does anything as drastic as cutting his vocal chords. Yet that's precisely what can happen to the barking dog. People do become violent and abusive, and take really extreme measures such as using inhumane shock collars, debarking him (i.e. cutting the vocal chords) or "getting rid of the dog." It's not necessary to do any of that to solve problem barking.

Dogs bark for lots of reasons. One of the reasons many people get dogs is because they offer a modicum of protection to home and family by barking to alert their humans to invaders on the property. Most anyone with the intent of doing harm won't risk being bitten by a dog. To stop the barking completely would be self-defeating.

Barking, in and of itself, is not a problem. A real problem exists when Sebastian starts barking at something, that something leaves and he continues barking. When dogs live their lives outdoors, all alone, they may become barkers just to hear the sound of their own voice. These are barking problems. Other problems exist, in these cases, that need solving. Why is Sebastian outside by himself all the time? Teaching him the *process of elimination* and house rules may be a solution. He wouldn't have to be exiled from the family life he desperately wants and needs.

When a family has a barking dog "problem," they must never ignore it. The vociferous canine can get the whole neighborhood up in arms, and the family becomes a bad reflection on all dog people. Ignoring the problem causes more unfair anti-dog legislation. Even avid dog lovers don't want to be kept awake by a neighbor's barking dog. The temporary solution is very simple. Bring Sebastian into the house! If he continues to bark, at least you're the only one bothered by him. That's fair! After all, he's your dog! Usually, bringing the dog inside with the family is enough to stop the barking.

If Sebastian must be outside during the day (although I cannot imagine why!) and neighbors complain about his barking, it's a good idea to ask them to help, if possible. Tell them you're aware of the problem. You don't intend to ignore it but you need their help. Ask them to keep a log of when the dog starts to bark, what is happening in the neighborhood at that time and what time he finally stops.

Now the angry neighbors can relax. First, they know that you're sincere about solving the problem and not ignoring their complaints. Second, the neighbors have something to do when the dog barks that makes them feel they're helping to solve the problem. Third, they begin to notice stimulants that cause the barking and become more aware of quiet periods. After all, no dog can bark 24 hours a day. Fourth, the information in this log is very helpful.

For example, if the barking starts at 2:30 every afternoon when children come home from school, then Sebastian shouldn't be where he can see the children. Maybe you could put up some additional fencing so he does not have access to the area where the children pass by. The fencing should not be chain link but rather something like redwood or pecky cedar. Sebastian should not be able to see the children through the fence.

You could hire a professional pet-sitter, responsible high schooler or retired person to come at 2:00 to put him in the house or garage until 3:30, take him for a walk or just keep him company for an hour to break up the long, boring day!

Whether or not Sebastian has a barking problem, it's a good idea to teach him to be quiet on command. You should always check to see what he's barking at. If it's a dangerous situation, let him continue to bark while you dial for help. If it's a friend or the delivery truck, you'd like him to stop barking when you say so.

Ironically, the first step in teaching Sebastian to be quiet on command is teach him to bark on command. This may seem contrary at first, but when he's barking at something, his attention is on that object. That's no time to teach him to be quiet! "Barking" an unknown word at him may appear to him that you are joining the barking! However, if you can make Sebastian bark on command, his attention will be on you. Then he can be taught a command word to stop the barking.

A good word for the bark command is **Defend!** The dog appears to be "protection trained." A stranger intending to harm you will be impressed and scared, but you and Sebastian know that you're just playing the **Barking** game.

It's not difficult to teach a bark command, especially when he's already a barker. Anytime he's barking, go to him with some treats in your hand, say **Defend! Good defend!,** feed him a treat and keep repeating this while he's barking. If he's not a barker, make him bark by tempting him with a treat or a toy while you stare directly into his eyes. Try making some "woofing" sounds as you do this. If he barks at the door bell or a knock on the door then ring the bell or make a knocking sound. Do anything that causes him to bark. When he makes any kind of a sound, tell him what he's doing while he's doing it and praise him! It's a command when you can say **Defend!** to a quiet dog and he barks. *Now* you can teach him to be quiet on command.

Get him into a barking mode—**Defend! Defend! Defend!** etc. Then put your index finger to your lips (a good hand signal) and say **Shush!** Gently hold his mouth closed, give a tidbit and say **Good Shush!** Repeat this and remove your hands from his snout as you count to two before you say **Good Shush!** and give a treat. Repeat it again and try counting to five. After a while, you shouldn't have to touch his snout to make him stop barking. He should stop when he sees the hand signal and hears **Shush!**

If your dog derives pleasure from barking, it's only fair to let him periodically experience this means of self-expression. Take him some place where his vocalizing won't disturb anyone and give him a "bark-a-thon." Give the **Defend** command. When he stops barking, tell him **Defend.** Do this until he's almost hoarse. Then he can get the barking out of his system and doesn't need to bark again for a week!

DIGGING

Most puppies go through a digging phase, then conveniently outgrow it if they are not left outdoors all the time. Some dogs, such as terriers and Northern breeds, never outgrow the behavior and individuals of any breed may be lifetime diggers. There are many reasons why dogs dig, and not all of them are solved by redirecting the digging.

Outdoor dogs may dig "cooling pits" in the summer and "warming pits" in the winter. In the summer, dogs dig "cooling pits" to lie in if proper shelter is not provided. Dogs perspire only through the pads of their feet. Their main cooling system is panting. The dog will stick his tongue out as far as possible and start to breathe hard. This causes evaporation of the fluid from his mouth, tongue and lungs. In this fashion the warm air in the lungs is exchanged for the cooler air in the mouth and the internal organs are cooled. It's a very exhausting, inefficient, possibly dehydrating way to keep cool!

If you have ever dug in the earth, you know that as you dig the earth becomes cooler. The dog digs a shallow pit, then lies with his belly on the earth to cool off his internal organs. It is comparable to lying on a cool tile floor in the middle of summer—it just feels good! In the winter, some dogs dig a warming pit by kicking the dirt into a mound that acts like a wind barrier, then huddling into the pit, shielded from the wind. Neither cooling pits nor warming pits are digging problems. Both are sheltering problems.

Another reason dogs dig is gophers in the yard. They can hear and smell the little critters and start "trenching" the yard in their pursuit. You don't have a

Digging ————————————————————

digging problem—you have a gopher problem. Eliminate the gophers and the digging will stop! Be sure not to use poisons or traps. You can stuff the gopher holes with "used" cat litter with the solids removed. Cats are natural enemies of gophers and the urine-scented litter is a safe, natural repellent.

Pregnant females dig whelping pits. When the mother dog is ready to give birth to the litter, she digs a pit as a nesting place. Dogs also dig under fences in order to get out. This is an escape problem caused by boredom, sterility of the environment, dogs on the other side of the fence, or for unaltered males and females, sexual urges.

If Sebastian is digging holes by the doors of the house, around the porch, under windows or next to the steps he is trying to dig his way back into the house. He is telling you something about himself—he misses you and wants to be with you.

Recreational digging is digging to bury things; digging to find things; or digging to pass the time of day. Digging is fun—people love to dig in their gardens to get the feel of the earth on their hands. It's a wonderful way to get in touch with nature. If Sebastian is allowed to watch you digging, he may get the idea you are teaching him that digging in the garden is good! Don't do your gardening when he can watch—put him where he cannot see you.

If your child were in the garden digging up your flowers, you wouldn't threaten to send her to an orphanage or fill the hole with water and hold her head underwater if she didn't stop. As a matter of fact, you probably wouldn't stop her from digging altogether. You most likely would get her a sandbox, then teach her to use it. That way she'd be able to have the fun of digging but you wouldn't worry about your garden being destroyed.

Do the same for Sebastian! It's not the digging that

upsets you—it's *where* he's digging that makes you
angry. Everyone probably has some place in the yard,
along one side of the house, an unused flower bed, etc.,
where the dog could safely dig clear to China! Find that
spot in your yard and clearly mark it with rocks,
bricks, wooden stakes, etc. If after a *sincere* effort to
find a pit in your yard, you cannot find one, consider
using a child's wading pool filled with earth. In either
case, prepare the soil by mixing some sand with it, to
make it nice and loose.

Now, play the **Digging** game at the designated
"digging pit" to teach Sebastian a new word—**Dig.** This
word means **dig** in your pit and only in your pit! You
must teach him this word first, so that later, when he
is caught in the act of digging any place but the pit, he
can be given an *instructive* reprimand.

With a handful of dog biscuits and a digging trowel,
invite Sebastian to **Come, Sit** and **Wait** by the "digging
pit." In plain view of him, place a biscuit in the pit,
sprinkle some earth on it and say **Dig!** When he gets
the treat say **Good dig!** Take another biscuit and cover
it with earth. Again say **Dig!** then **Good dig!** when he
unearths it. With the hand trowel, make a little hole,
bury another treat, release Sebastian with **Dig!** and
praise him with **Good dig!**

Play this game for five minutes at a time as often as
you like. The more often the **Digging** game is played,
the sooner Sebastian learns what **Dig!** means. When he
is doing something else in the yard, say **Dig!** If he runs
to his pit, **Dig!** has become a usable command.

Now comes the hard part. You must catch Sebastian
in the act of digging anywhere but the pit in order to
give an instructive reprimand. The silliest thing I ever
heard to accomplish this was to attach a long cord to
the dog's collar, then walk him around the yard, wait
for him to dig and reprimand him. I am sure that if I
ever attempted to do this with my dog I would grow

very old and still never catch him digging. Most dogs don't need to dig when someone is around. It's an activity that helps to pass the long, lonely hours the dog must spend alone in the yard.

The most fun way to catch him in the act of digging is to have an indoor-dog-teaching party. Invite friends, family or neighbors over for a pizza party. First, your entire family must leave the house, including driving away and parking out of hearing range. Then, very quietly sneak back into the house and leave the door unlocked. Instruct your guests not to knock or ring the bell but just come right in.

With Sebastian outside, everyone takes a 15 minute shift of watching him from a strategic location in the house, where he can be carefully observed without being aware that he is being watched. Take only 15 minute watches because watching a dog sleep is very boring and you will get a reputation for throwing very bad parties!

When someone catches him in the act of digging any place but the pit, everyone runs outside screaming **AHHHHHHHHHHHHHHHHHHHHH! Dig!** When Sebastian goes to the pit, he's lavishly praised with **Good dig!**

This "sandbox" for the dog works especially well if you periodically bury dog cookies, chew toys, etc., in the digging pit. When Sebastian digs anyplace else he finds roots, rocks and trouble. But when he digs in his pit, he has a treasure trove. He never knows what marvelous surprise awaits him but he knows the surprises are found only in the pit.

The best solutions for most digging problems are spaying/neutering, becoming more involved with the dog, including him in your activities and bringing him into your home. Teach him the rules of the house. Help him to be an acceptable family member who can be trusted alone indoors.

Living With A Dog

A HOME WITHOUT A DOG IS JUST A HOUSE

The reason most dogs live in the yard is because people are lazy. It is really deplorable that so many people bring home a puppy, then don't follow through and build a relationship with their pet so they can enjoy the dog that the puppy grew up to be. They may take him to obedience classes but they rarely spend any time together after graduating. The poor dog ends up alone in the yard because the owner just "can't be bothered" to continue the dog's education.

Rather than teach the dog the rules of the house it seems easier to just "put the dog outside." Anyone not willing to assume their part of the relationship should seriously reconsider obtaining a dog. The family must accept accountability for their dog's behavior and take the time to teach him how to live indoors as a member of the family.

A dog living in the home with the family is the most rewarding experience of all for both the dog and the people. The benefits of having Sebastian can only be obtained if you spend time with him. A dog living in the yard is just too easy to forget. But the dog in the house is a family member—he cannot be forgotten or ignored. He is with you, so you are always teaching him new words and rules and he is always learning.

He can teach you about forgiveness, accentuating the positive, having fun and unconditional love. He is a protector of home and family and a comforting presence when you are alone or not feeling well. By sharing your life and your home with Sebastian you enrich your life and his, because you can quickly and easily teach him to be a well-mannered family member.

It is not difficult to teach him "house manners" but first he must know the *process of elimination* and be taught about chewing. However, there is more to living in the house than just knowing that the toilet is outside and the sofa is not a chew toy.

Sebastian needs to know what behavior is appropriate in any given situation. It is up to you to teach him the rules of your home by setting up the circumstances before they actually occur, because when they do happen for real, you are pre-occupied with what is going on and not paying close attention to Sebastian. Teaching should be done in staged set-ups; that way you can concentrate on Sebastian and, if he screws up, you can give an immediate instructive reprimand as to what he should have done. Then your house can be a home with a well-mannered, informed family pet.

Sebastian can live a more normal life as part of a social group. He can feel safe and secure in knowing that you, the leader, will be in charge. He will ask nothing more of you than to feed him, groom him, teach him the rules, exercise him, play with him, care for him when he is sick, and love him. As payment for all of that, he will respect you, obey you, warn you of intruders, protect you, amuse you, and bring you joy, laughter, comfort, companionship and nonjudgmental adulation!

"STAY" FOR DINNER!

If Sebastian is to have freedom in the house and not spend his life confined to the kitchen, laundry room or yard, he must be taught how to behave in normal family situations. When the family is eating meals, most people put the dog outside rather than teach him to **Stay** nicely in the house. The problem is mealtime becomes a signal to Sebastian that he is about to be isolated from the family—remember, isolation is the

AMF

most severe form of punishment to a dog. His behavior may become unpleasant as mealtime approaches because he doesn't want to be "put outside." Who can blame him? The family comes to the table to enjoy food and time together and he is always excluded from this family gathering. Take the time to teach him how to behave at mealtime. It is very simple to do.

The family must agree that, during the teaching, mealtime may be a bit strange but it is well worth the effort. Sebastian should be taught to **Stay** in the kitchen or dining area. I think it is easier to teach him to **Down** and **Stay** in the dining area, because he is closer, easier to keep an eye on and can be quickly reprimanded if he breaks the **Stay.**

If you decide to have him in the other room, put up a temporary barrier that he can see through—it could be as simple as a cord stretched across the doorway. Dogs are territorial and very spatially oriented. The barrier is more for you than Sebastian. It is so you can immediately see when he has crossed the boundary. Place him on the other side of the barrier and tell him to **Down** and **Stay.** As you walk away, keep an eye on him to be sure he isn't moving. If he moves, reprimand him and again tell him to **Down** and **Stay.** Keep repeating this until you can get all the way to the dining table and actually sit down. Then go back to Sebastian and praise him—**Good stay!** Now repeat the process and remain seated at the table for longer and longer periods, each time going back to him and praising him.

When the family is seated at the table, someone must be responsible for *watching the dog,* to immediately reprimand him if he moves. Dinner conversation may be a bit crazy for a while because this person may periodically interrupt the conversation to reprimand Sebastian and tell him to **Down** and **Stay.** But it's only for a few meals and then he understands that when the family or anyone is seated at the dining table, he must **Down** and **Stay** in his place. Before long you won't have to command him; just seeing you sit at the table becomes a signal for him to assume the **Down position** and **Stay** where he belongs until released.

Never allow anyone to feed Sebastian from the table. Spicy foods can upset their system and/or cause misbehavior such as "begging." Be especially cautious if there are small children at the table who might drop or sneak food to him. If you give Sebastian leftovers, always place the food in his bowl and feed him in his usual place. That way, Sebastian can be a welcome "guest" at any meal!

WHO'S THAT KNOCKING AT MY DOOR?!?

Another area of concern for most owners is the front door. Most dogs are never taught how to behave when someone knocks at the door. Actually, most people don't really think about how they want the dog to behave when visitors come calling. The only time they realize a problem exists is when someone is at the door, they are yelling at the hysterically barking dog and utter chaos reigns!

When you put Sebastian outside or in another room

while you visit with your guest, he perceives himself as isolated from the family. Isolation is a very severe form of punishment to Sebastian, so every time someone approaches the door and knocks, his door behavior becomes worse and worse. From the dog's point of view, he knows he will be severely punished (isolated) if that person is allowed inside the house. He becomes more and more out of control at the sound of a knock or the ring of the doorbell, trying to chase the intruder away so he won't be forced to suffer isolation.

Take the time to teach Sebastian door manners and he won't act like a maniac—he'll make you very proud instead. Teaching makes the difference between an out-of-control dog and a confident one who knows the appropriate behavior for a given circumstance.

The best time to teach "door manners" is in a set-up situation, before the actual event, so you can focus all of your attention on Sebastian. Then, when someone visits for real, Sebastian will know the rules of the door. The teaching is done in steps. Be certain Sebastian is consistently successful and confident on each step before progressing to the next one. If you experience problems with any step, always back up to the last one that worked and attempt to proceed at a slower pace.

1. STAY—Sebastian must be able to **Stay,** so this is where you begin. Be sure he understands the **Stay** and succeeds every time.

2. Sebastian must be able to **Stay** while you walk away from him in any direction. You can walk to the left, to the right, from the front, to the back, all around him and he stays until you come back and release him.

3. Now comes the most important **Stay.** You must be able to walk away from Sebastian *with your back to him.* Thus far you may have practiced **Stay** by walking away facing the dog. It is more difficult when your back is turned because you cannot see him and he cannot see your face. At first, it will help to look over your

OH GOOD BOY...
ARE YOU NAPPING?

AMF

shoulder to be sure he **stays.** If he tries to follow you, give a quick verbal reprimand, place him back in his **stay** and keep on trying. Don't progress too far away too quickly. Just a step at a time, until you can walk all the way to the door.

4. Now Sebastian is taught to remain in the **Stay** through the sound of a knock or a ringing bell. Tell Sebastian to **Sit** and **Stay,** then you knock on the floor, a table or anything close to him or ring the bell. Then gradually move the sound further away until it is at the door. He must continue to **Stay** all through the knocking or ringing.

5. Next, add your voice. Sebastian is in a **stay,** you

knock on the door or ring the bell, go back to the dog and say "Who's there?", "Just a minute!" or whatever you normally say when guests arrive. Say this while standing next to him, then gradually add some distance until you are saying it at the door.

6. For this step you need the help of a friend. Tell Sebastian to **Sit** and **Stay,** your friend knocks on the door, you say "Just a minute!", your friend comes in and stands by the door. Repeat this over and over, gradually allowing your friend to take one step, then two steps, etc., toward the dog.

7. This is the final stage. When someone comes to the door, Sebastian is usually running around the house free, not already in a **Stay.** Have your friend knock on the door. When the dog comes running tell him to **Sit! Good sit! Stay!** Repeat this over and over until the knock itself almost becomes a signal for Sebastian to go to the door, **Sit** and **Stay.** Then answer the door. Your friend comes in, slowly approaches the dog, gives him a pat or a treat and sits down. You can release Sebastian from the **Stay** at an appropriate time.

With this approach you teach the dog how to behave in stages and set-ups, so when the real event occurs he will eventually know the rules. While you are in the process of teaching these seven steps, it is advisable to always have a leash at the front door. That way, when friends come calling for real, you can quickly snap the leash on Sebastian and tell him to **Sit! Good Sit! Stay!** With the leash on him, you are in control and he cannot be an obnoxious pest at the door. Keep the leash on him during the entire visit if necessary and practice a long **Stay** in the **Down** position. By doing all of this, you create a dog with manners who doesn't need to be thrown outside when company arrives.

Another facet of door manners is to teach Sebastian to **Sit** and **Wait** at a door until he is invited into the room. You accomplish several things by doing this.

First, you are the dog's *leader*, so you should *lead* the dog into the room, not follow him. Second, if your dog knows that he should **Sit** and **Wait** at a door to be invited in, you don't have to trip over him at the door when your arms are full of groceries, laundry, tool boxes, etc. Third, if your dog **Sits** and **Waits** at all doors, you will be less likely to suffer the pain and sorrow of a dog that runs out the front door into the street and gets killed by a car.

The teaching is very simple. Just walk around your house with Sebastian and every time you come to a doorway tell him to **Sit** and **Wait**. Remember to use **Wait,** not **Stay,** because you are not going to return to Sebastian to release him. Then you walk into the room and release him with whatever release word you have chosen (OK, All Right, Free, etc.). If he tries to enter the room with you, ahead of you or before you say the release word, verbally reprimand him, place him back on his side of the door, firmly tell him **Sit! Wait!** then proceed into the room. In the beginning, don't have him **wait** for a long period to be released. Remember, you want him to succeed and this is something new. Once he has caught on to the idea, he'll probably **Sit** and **Wait** automatically at all doors until he is politely invited to join you in the room. At new doors, you may have to say the commands but he'll obey quickly.

There is no excuse for Sebastian not to be allowed in the home. You teach him the rules and his command words so you can communicate with him. Why teach him words and then never talk to him? The words **Sit, Down, Walk, Come, Stay, Wait** and **Off** are the basis for helping Sebastian to learn how to behave in or out of the house.

IF YOU LOVE 'EM, LEASH 'EM

Since you taught Sebastian to **Walk** nicely on a leash, you can take him with you on an evening stroll, to the mailbox, to play sessions with other puppies, etc. The oddest thing is that people teach the word **Walk** then never say it to the dog again. They take him out on a leash, and he pulls them; they tug at him but they don't think to put their hand down by the dog's face and say **Walk.** Why teach him the word if you aren't going to use it when walking the dog? Going for a **walk** with your best friend should be a bright spot in the day for both of you!

It's a good idea to teach Sebastian to **Wait** when you stop walking. Move the hand that's signaling **Walk** up and across your chest. Bring your other hand over and move as you did when you taught the **Stay.** Say **Wait! Good wait!** and give the reward. Do this every time, and going through the gates or doors won't be chaotic. He can stop and **Wait** while you unlatch the gate or unlock the door. Don't have him **Sit** and **Wait** because he may **Sit** on an anthill or the ground may be wet or muddy and it is very unpleasant to **Sit** under those conditions.

Another appropriate thing to do when walking is teach Sebastian to **Wait** when you come to the curb. Tell him **Wait!** Look both ways before crossing, then say **Walk** when all is clear. That way he doesn't drag you across the street, endangering both your lives. Eventually the curb may become a signal to **Wait** and if Sebastian is ever loose (which should never happen), hopefully he would stop and **Wait** at the curb before crossing the street—it just might save his life!

Remember this—when you are walking Sebastian, you are the most boring thing about the walk for him. He is already familiar with how you smell, sound, move, etc. All the trees, bushes, fire hydrants, telephone poles, fences, sidewalks, yards, children, dogs, cats, people and everything else along your route are far more interesting because they are new. It is up to you to keep Sebastian interested enough in you that

he wants to stay with you. Don't be a boring, silent grouch. You are on a walk with your best friend, let him know how happy that makes you. Talk to him or sing to him—he'll love it!

One last thing on this subject. It seems that too many people want to be able to walk the dog off-leash. I personally don't understand why anyone would want to do that. It is so extremely dangerous. I don't care how well you think you have taught your dog—he is a dog and that is all he is capable of being. He has doggy instincts to chase after moving objects such as cats, squirrels, children, cars, bicycles and any loose animals.

It takes only a few seconds to snap on a leash and that action can mean the difference between life and death. Our cities and towns are over-crowded with automobiles, people and pets—that is why there are leash laws everywhere. It is illegal in most communities for dogs to be off-leash on public property. A dog on a leash is safe, secure, under control and legal. Leashing Sebastian is not cruel—it is evidence of how much you love him. A leashed dog is a loved dog!

WANTED: DELIGHTFUL TRAVELLING COMPANION

Travelling in the car is another area where Sebastian should be taught your rules. He should not be allowed to freely wander around inside a vehicle or stick his head out a window. A pebble kicked up by a car in front of you is speeding like a bullet, and could actually kill a dog with his head out the window. Many dogs are injured by flying objects penetrating the eyes, ears, nose, mouth or head.

The best way to travel with Sebastian is to have him crated inside the vehicle or secured by a seat belt and restraining harness. If this is not possible, have him **Down** and **Stay** on the back floor. Again, this is not always possible as not all cars have a back seat. The next best thing would be **Down** on the floor on the passenger side. This too is not always an option. If all of the above recommendations don't work for you, have him **Stay** on the back seat or passenger seat. Regardless of where Sebastian is he should be taught to **Stay** while in the car.

You cannot teach car manners while you are driving—that is too dangerous. The best time to teach Sebastian about the car is when you do not have to go anywhere. When the car is parked in the garage or driveway, **walk** him on-leash to the car, tell him to **Sit** and **Wait,** then open the door. If he jumps in before he is released, quickly pull him back out, close the door and command him to **Sit** and **Wait.** He must learn not to jump into the car until you release him. Keep repeating this until Sebastian reliably **waits** for you to tell him it's OK and doesn't bolt into the car.

If he is to be crated, place the crate in the car with the crate door open and release him with the word **Crate!** (a command he learned during crate teaching). Remember to remove his leash while he is in the crate. If his crate is too big to fit in your car then show him where he must go by placing a treat or favorite toy in that location so that he is drawn to the desired spot. Then tell him to **Sit** or **Down** and **Stay.**

Next you get into the car and just sit there. If he moves from his spot, correct him, put him back where he belongs and tell him firmly to **Stay!** Keep repeating this until he **stays** there for a few minutes with no trouble.

Now teach him about getting out of the car—be sure his leash is attached to his collar before the door is opened. Sebastian must **wait** until you release him. Open the car door; if he is in a crate, open the crate door as well and say **Wait!** If he tries to bolt out of the car, push him back to his place or crate and tell him firmly to **Wait.** He must not be allowed to bolt out of the car or jump over you to get out first just because the door is open. If he jumps into traffic he may cause an accident or possibly be killed by a passing car. You must be able to open the door and know Sebastian will **wait** to be invited out of the car. Accomplish this before you move on to the next step.

With Sebastian in a **Stay** in his place, get into the car, turn on the engine and back down the driveway. If he moves, stop and give a correction. When he **stays** where he belongs as you go up and down the driveway, try going to the corner of the street. Drive slowly and carefully. Be prepared to pull to the curb if a correction should be necessary. If you have a friend who can drive while you watch Sebastian, that is even better. A dog taught car manners is a delightful travelling companion.

THE CANINE SENIOR CITIZEN

Living with a senior citizen dog is a mixed blessing. If your dog has lived into the senior years, give yourself a pat on the back. You have taken excellent care of Sebastian by feeding him properly, teaching him his lessons, exercising him, loving him and taking him to the veterinarian for yearly examinations and treatment when necessary.

As your dog ages, you may notice some changes, such as less eating, more drinking, frequent urination, less activity, sleeping more of the time, a little slower moving, stiffness, disease-proneness, irritability, etc. These are normal changes that many of us experience with age.

These changes occur gradually and you probably won't notice most of them right away—only when you compare the dog to what he used to do. You will probably make adjustments to these situations by feeding him a quality geriatric diet two or three times a day, taking shorter and/or slower walks, letting him in and out more frequently, filling the water bowl more often, giving him a softer orthopedic bed for his tender joints, not disturbing him, taking him to the veterinarian every six months for check-ups or at the first sign of any changes, etc.

Sometimes, as dogs age, they develop physical problems that require you to make further changes to their lifestyles.

BLINDNESS

As your dog ages you may notice a cloudiness developing in the iris of his eyes. It is usually nothing to worry about and rarely causes any problems with the dog's vision. Actually, blindness is not as severe a handicap for dogs as it is for humans. Of all the human senses, sight is the one people seem to depend on most heavily; and when they lose vision, people have a very difficult time adjusting.

A dog, on the other hand, actually depends more on his senses of smell and hearing and adjusts rather quickly to loss of sight. The loss is usually gradual and the dog has time to make adjustments.

You may notice him bumping into things at times, but for the most part he gets around rather well by moving more slowly, navigating the borders of a room, keeping his head down so that he can sniff the pathway and if he does bump something, he hits it with his hard head, not his sensitive snout.

Since the dog is very scent oriented, you can try to help by spraying a distinctive scent on objects to forewarn him of their presence. However, having lived with several blind dogs, I have found the most important thing is not to rearrange furniture and objects in the rooms the dog goes into. A blind dog seems to have a mental picture of the layout, and once familiar with the room, avoids bumping into things as well as a sighted dog would.

I have also found that adding a few new words, to alert him to situations, is very helpful. For example, when walking with my blind dog, I am his "Seeing Eye" person, so I help as much as possible. When we come to a curb or a bump or a step I say **Up! Good up!** to climb it or **Careful! Good careful!** when going down. When he approaches objects he might bump into, I say **Whoops!** and he soon learns to swerve away from where he is heading. On a **Come,** I always clap my hands or stomp my feet to help guide him to me. When he does **come** to me, I always reach out to touch him as I continue talking to him. Since he cannot see me, it is reassuring to him to hear my voice and feel my touch. I use touch a lot to guide him in the house and in strange places. It requires a little extra thought to live with a blind dog, but it is really worth it.

DEAFNESS

Often an older dog does not hear as well as he used to. He usually can hear some sounds but not others. One advantage to a dog's becoming deaf is that he no longer has panic attacks during thunderstorms and Fourth of July fireworks. It is not impossible to communicate with a deaf dog.

Sometimes talking in a higher voice helps (although some dogs will respond better to a lower voice). Talk a little louder but don't shout, just be sure you enunciate your words clearly. Along with deafness is a tendency for words to sound mumbled when spoken at normal volume, and the dog appears not to understand simple words.

Most importantly, if you have taught your dog with the techniques in this book, you have a great way to communicate with a deaf dog—hand signals! I always recommend using voice and hand signals together throughout the dog's life. That way he is familiar with both means of communication. Also, touching him is a great way to get his attention focused on you. It is most important that your deaf dog never be too far away from you—you cannot *call* him back. He has to be close by and always paying attention to you.

INCONTINENCE

You will notice that your older dog drinks more water—that is typical but it can also be a sign of kidney problems, diabetes and other problems. Therefore, it behooves you to visit the veterinarian when you realize you are filling the water bowl a lot more than before.

Along with consuming more water, your dog will urinate more frequently—what goes in, must come out! When you are home, of course your dog will probably let you know when he needs to go outside, but when you are gone, you may come back to a puddle (or a pile). Your dog is not being naughty, he is just not physically capable of holding his bladder or bowel for long periods of time because his sphincter muscles and back end are losing tone and strength.

When a dog suffers bladder incontinence, most

people attempt to deal with it by withholding water. This is a very bad idea—the dog needs more water to filter through the kidneys because his systems do not operate as efficiently as they used to. Withholding water can actually endanger the dog's health.

A dog suffering from bowel incontinence may also have accidents. It is very important to ensure that the dog does not have loose stool or diarrhea at any time.

Feed him a high-quality food and just enough of it to form firm stool. Older dogs need less food because they are less active, and often have poor appetites since their sense of smell has weakened and the food does not seem as appealing. If this happens, you can try feeding steamed brown rice mixed with cottage cheese, boiled chicken or boiled hamburger to stimulate his appetite and keep the stool firm.

If your dog becomes incontinent, you may want to make some changes to his lifestyle. It is easier if carpeted areas are off-limits and the dog is confined to tile or linoleum-floored rooms. He should still be able to see and hear you—after all, you don't want him to feel isolated. His bedding should be made of easily washable material and placed out of the flow of traffic, but in a comfortable spot where he is still included in family gatherings. Have lots of stain and odor remover on hand to clean up accidents, as well as some gentle, no-rinse pet shampoo to clean up the dog when necessary.

Living with an incontinent dog is entirely possible with a little forethought and planning. Yes, it is a bit more work but after all the years of joy, love and companionship your dog has given you, maybe now it's your turn to give him some comfort in return.

IRRITABILITY

Older dogs do seem to be more easily irritated. It is probably because of some stiffness, arthritis, lameness, deafness, blindness, etc. If you notice that your dog is slower moving, hard to awaken and a little stiffer, then you have probably noticed some irritability as well. Obviously, you should avoid doing those things that annoy him. Yes, I know you are the leader, but there comes a time when you have to just respect the aged.

Make your irritable senior citizen's life comfortable and avoid, as much as possible, the situations that cause him discomfort. Take shorter and slower walks—*always* use your leash, his reflexes are much slower than they used to be. If your dog has spent most of his life outdoors, now you *must* bring him inside. He is more affected by changes in the temperature and is less able to regulate his own body temperature.

The older dog may suffer from arthritis, stiffness, pain upon moving and some muscle atrophy. He will be slow and cranky when startled or awakened. Have your veterinarian recommend whatever treatment she may prescribe to control the pain and discomfort, and give him lots of tender loving care and affection.

Sometimes older dogs appear to be more dependent than they used to be. They hover around you—always wanting to be where you are and as close to you as possible. They may show fear at new things, new situations, or new people and appear to want to crawl into your skin for safety. If this happens, do not take the dog with you when you go to places he has never been. If you bring some new object into the home, place it where the dog does not have access. When there are new people around, you must be very friendly and jovial to them so the dog will see you as happy and relaxed. Your attitude will help him know he can relax with this person. These are simple concessions to make in order for your dog to enjoy his golden years.

EUTHANASIA

Of course the most difficult part of seeing your dog getting older is the realization that your time together is going to end. Everyone hopes the dog will die painlessly and peacefully in his sleep, but that very rarely happens. Usually it is up to the family to make a final decision.

Most books and friends will probably tell you if the dog is in pain and/or has no quality of life you should euthanize him, and that is probably true. However, I prefer to give the family permission to know the right time in their heart of hearts. If the relationship between the family and the dog has been close and strong, they—and only they—will know the precise time to say their last farewell to their beloved pet.

Many people might say you are "waiting too long and being selfish"; "he's just responding out of habit"; "he doesn't have a life worth living"; "he's suffering"; etc. Who cares what others say? This dog is part of your family and you must not feel rushed, forced, pressured or guilty when you decide to take this irreversible step.

Well-meaning friends may try to counsel you to do it before you are ready. They are not cold or unfeeling, but rather your pain and anguish over this decision probably makes them uncomfortable and they think that they are helping by reminding you that you can "always get another dog." That may very well be true but you cannot get another Sebastian. In all the time the universe has been, and will be, there has never before been a Sebastian and there never will be again. There is only one of each of us for all eternity.

There is no formula to determine the proper time to euthanize a pet—it's just a gut-level feeling, like a message between the dog and the family that they are now ready to say good-bye to each other. The decision of euthanasia should involve every family member old enough to understand what is going to happen. Children should not be excluded and then told the pet ran away—they may feel guilt or fear about what has happened to him. Dying is a very real part of living and this can be a very informative, helpful, special time for a child to learn that old age and dying do not have to be scary and ugly.

I have found that having a pet euthanized at home is less traumatic for the family, and more importantly, less stressful for the pet. An old sick dog does not need the stress of a last car ride to the veterinary hospital with its odd smells, needles, noise, chaos, etc. It is very important, if you are planning to stay with the pet, that you be as relaxed and calm as possible. Remember that your dog takes his cues from you and your calm attitude will help him to relax and feel comfortable. After it is over, you can break down.

It is perfectly healthy and normal to feel the same intensity of emotion over the death of a pet as over the death of a human. After all, your dog was a family member; like a child who never grew up, he never left home, he always needed you and now you realize just how much you needed him. Give yourself time and permission to grieve. If you feel that you cannot cope with the grief alone, involve the family—let everyone share their memories and their feelings of joy and sorrow. It always helps to know you are not alone in this big, cold world.

If nothing seems to help and you just cannot get over the grief, do not hesitate to contact a counselor. Moira Anderson's book *Coping with Sorrow on the Loss of Your Pet* may be helpful in dealing with your grief.

A brief word is appropriate about obtaining another pet. Many well-intentioned friends and family often want to get you a new puppy right away. They think this will help you forget and get on with your life. Inform them, in no uncertain terms, that they must *not* do this. If you have not finished the grieving process, you will probably resent a new puppy trying to take your dog's place, using his toys, bowls, bed, etc.

Tell your friends that you will get another dog when you are ready and not one minute before. Besides, since the dog is going to live with you, you should have the joy and honor of choosing (and being chosen by) your next canine best friend!

Sometimes the grief that people suffer over the loss of a pet makes them feel that they do not want another dog ever again. They feel that the pain of old age and saying good-bye was just too devastating to ever have to experience with another dog. I feel that these people must be stuck somewhere in the grieving process. It seems to me it is an insult to the memory of a deceased pet and a denial of all he unquestioningly gave to you, to never want to experience that joy again. You definitely honor the belated pet's memory by wanting to again share your life, home, joy, heart and love with a new pet. It says that all he gave to you was so wonderful that you do not want to be without the companionship of a dog again. After all, compared to all the years of companionship, joy, fun and unconditional love, the time spent with old age and euthanasia is only a brief moment.

CONCLUSION

Because you have taught Sebastian how to behave in your home, around company, on a walk, in the car, etc., you can now live with a dog who is a true companion. The more you use words and practice with your dog, the better behaved he will be. He can be welcomed as a member of the family and probably understands and obeys rules better than your own children!

A dog who lives in the house with the family is always learning. Teaching is never over because he is always with you. He presents many opportunities each day for you to use the words you so carefully taught him, as well as new words for new situations. Because he is always present, he learns more and more each day. Your dog has been taught how to learn and that learning is fun.

Both of you can enjoy each other and learn from each other. You can live with a dog who behaves like an educated pet, rather than a pest, and your dog doesn't have to live in fear of you. He knows that if he screws up, you will not inflict pain on him, but rather respect his point of view and instruct him so that he can learn the appropriate behavior for the given situation.

Living happily with any pet requires that you become informed and educated and love and respect your dog. Understand that he has a point of view that is probably different from yours. Just because something is different does not mean that it is wrong—it's just different! If you are consistent, fair, dependable and able to see things from the dog's point of view, you can solve your doggy problems quickly and easily. After all, your dog really does want to please you.

Reward your dog for the many things that he does correctly and he will want to repeat what makes you happy. It's up to you to make sure your dog understands the message you are trying to send. Make your house a home by teaching Sebastian the rules and letting him be a part of your family. The other family members are not beaten, thrown outside, chained, "gotten rid of" or choked when they make mistakes. So, let's stop choking dogs and start teaching, understanding, respecting, enjoying and loving them!

Appendix

Some purebred dog owners register their dogs with a national kennel club. For more information write to:

American Kennel Club
51 Madison Avenue
New York, NY 10010

Australian National Kennel
   Council
Royal Show Grounds
Epsom Road
Ascot Vale
Victoria 3032 Australia

Canadian Kennel Club
2150 Bloor Street West
Toronto
Ontario M65 4V7
Canada

Fédération Cynologique
   Internationale
(International Canine
   Federation)
Rue Léopold - II
14-6530 Thuin
Belgium

Kennel Union of Southern
   Africa
6th Floor, Bree Castle
68 Bree Street
Cape Town 8001
South Africa

New Zealand Kennel Club
31 Pirie Street
Wellington
New Zealand

States Kennel Club
P.O. Box 389
Hattiesburg, MS 39403-0389

The Kennel Club
1 Clarges Street
Piccadilly
London W.1. Y8AB

United Kennel Club
100 East Kilgore Road
Kalamazoo, MI 49001-5598

Index

Index

All-Breed Dog Books From T.F.H.

H-1106, 544 pp
Over 400 color photos

H-1091, 2 Vols., 912 pp
Over 1100 color photos

TS-175, 896 pp
Over 1300 color photos

The T.F.H. all-breed dog books are the most comprehensive and colorful of all dog books available. The most famous of these recent publications, *The Atlas of Dog Breeds of the World,* written by Dr. Bonnie Wilcox and Chris Walkowicz, is now available as a two-volume set. Now in its fourth edition, the *Atlas* remains one of the most sought-after gift books and reference works in the dog world.

A very successful spinoff of the *Atlas* is the *Mini-Atlas of Dog Breeds,* written by Andrew De Prisco and James B. Johnson. This compact but comprehensive book has been praised and recommended by most national dog publications for its utility and reader-friendliness. The true field guide for dog lovers.

Canine Lexicon by the authors of the *Mini-Atlas* is an up-to-date encyclopedic dictionary for the dog person. It is the most complete single volume on the dog ever published covering more breeds than any other book as well as other relevant topics, including health, showing, training, breeding, anatomy, veterinary terms, and much more. No dog book before has ever offered this many stunning color photographs of all breeds, dog sports, and topics (over 1300 in full color!).

More Dog Books from
T.F.H. Publications, Inc.

H-1016, 224 pp
135 photos

H-969, 224 pp
62 color photos

H-1061, 608 pp
Black/white photos

TS-101, 192 pp
Over 100 photos

TS-130, 160 pp
50 color illustra.

TW-102, 256 pp
Over 200 color

TW-113, 256 pp
200 color photos

H-962, 255 pp
Nearly 100 photos

SK-044, 64 pp
Over 50 color

KW-227, 96 pp
Nearly 100 color

PS-872, 240 pp
178 color illustrations

H-1095, 272 pp
Over 160 color illustrations

PS-607, 254 pp
136 Black/white photos